All Israel Shall Be Saved

Jill Curry

All Israel Shall be Saved
Praying for the Redemption of Israel

Jewish and Israel Prayer Focus 2020 - 5801

I do not want you to be ignorant of this mystery, brothers and sisters, so that you may not be conceited: Israel has experienced a hardening in part until the full number of the Gentiles has come in, and in this way all Israel will be saved. Rom 11:11-26a (NIV)

Front cover painting and design: Jennifer Marshall
http://www.lighthorseart.com.au

Copyright © 2020 J.M. Curry. All rights reserved

This book or any portion thereof may not be reproduced or used in any manner whatsoever without the express written permission of the publisher except for the use of brief quotation in a book review.

First printing 2020
ISBN 978-0-9945758-2-1

Unless otherwise noted, Scripture quotations taken from the New American Standard Bible® (NASB), Copyright © 1960, 1962, 1963, 1968, 1971, 1972, 1973, 1975, 1977, 1995 by The Lockman Foundation. Used by permission. http://www.lockman.org

Scripture quotations marked (NIV) are taken from the Holy Bible, New International Version®, NIV®. Copyright © 1973, 1978, 1984, 2011 by Biblica, Inc.™ Used by permission of Zondervan. All rights reserved worldwide. https://www.zondervan.com. The "NIV" and "New International Version" are trademarks registered in the United States Patent and Trademark Office by Biblica, Inc.™

Email: watchmen777@optusnet.com.au
Website: http://jewishandisraelprayerfocus.org. Donations can be made through this website.
Post: PO Box 54, Kerrimuir, VIC 3129 Australia

The *Jewish and Israel Prayer Focus* is a sub-entity of Living Way Christian Network Inc. Cheques should be made out to 'Living Way Christian Network'. Profits from the sale of books go to support Messianic Jewish and Arab Christian congregations and ministries in Israel.

Endorsements

Over the years many of us have read through the annual *Jewish Prayer Focus* as a tool for intercession during the biblical High Holy days.

Jill Curry has now given us a rich resource of information to use in prayer throughout the year. She outlines the historical and prophetic background of Israel and the calling of the Gentile nations to fulfil their destiny in God's end time Kingdom plan, according to His prophetic timeline.

This is balanced writing, easy to read and comes from an experienced author who is well equipped to write on this subject. Most importantly the author firmly answers the question, 'Why pray for the Jewish people?'

Jenny Hagger, AM, Founder and Director, Australian House of Prayer for all Nations and Mission World Aid, Senior Pastor Father's House, Adelaide, South Australia

----

Many Christians world-wide are coming into a revelation of the Father's heart for Israel, the Jewish people, and the central place Jerusalem has in His heart and plans. They desire to pray for Israel and for Jerusalem, but don't know where to begin. Jill's book is a powerful and wonderfully balanced guide to daily prayer for Israel. She does a great job at giving a prayer focus for each month with an overview of Israeli and Jewish life through the biblical feasts and holidays important to the history of modern Israel, which she shares from first-hand experience that comes through living among the Jewish people here in Israel. Along with the prayer focus for the month, there is a relevant Scripture to pray each day. This is more than a very good book to gain understanding. It is a valuable guide to help you pray daily for the apple of God's eye with cultural, spiritual, and Scriptural insight.

Rick Ridings, Founder (together with his wife Patricia) of Succat Hallel,

All Israel Shall be Saved

24/7 House of Worship and Prayer in Jerusalem overlooking the Temple Mount. International Speaker, and Author (together with his wife Patricia) of the book: Shifting Nations through Houses of Prayer

---

Author Jill Curry has done a great service to the Body of Messiah by compiling eighteen years of the *Jewish and Israel Prayer Focus* material into one new book *All Israel Shall Be Saved*. Jill has made this material accessible and understandable and this book is a both a great introduction to those who want to know more about the Feasts of Israel as well as a valuable resource to those who have already been praying for Israel and the Jewish people. I commend Jill Curry for her 'labour of love' for God and the Jewish people.

Lawrence Hirsch, Executive Director of Celebrate Messiah and Rabbi of Beit HaMashiach Congregation, Melbourne, Australia

---

Needless to say, we are living in historic times, times that require understanding of G-d's calling to us personally and corporately. Central to every Christian's calling is G-d's enduring covenant with both the Land and the children of Israel. From Genesis to Revelation is woven a consistent message of encouragement that 'all Israel shall be saved.'

With this unique resource, Jill Curry has created more than just a prayer book. The content is so rich, allowing it to serve as an excellent daily devotional and/or Bible study connecting the community of faith in and around the world to pray and support G-d's plan for Israel.

Saturated with multiple opportunities to better understand and respond to G-d's calling in your life regarding Israel, I highly recommend this incredible resource.

Bishop Robert Stearns
Executive Director, Eagles' Wings, New York
Founder and Co-Chairman, Day of Prayer for the Peace of Jerusalem

About the author:

Jill Curry has a Masters in Higher Education, a Bachelor of Music and a Diploma of Ministry. She founded Shnat Ratzon Ministries (Year of the Lord's Favour) in 1998 as an Israel Intercessory Support Ministry. From 1997-2001 she lived in Israel, teaching at the 'School of Worship' in Jerusalem, and researching and writing *Prepare the Way for the King of Glory* with Tom Hess. The Jewish and Israel Prayer Focus was birthed in 2002 from Australia, to pray for the Jewish people and to introduce Christians to the Lord's biblical Feasts, as well as sharing the good news of God's redemptive work amongst the Jewish people. Of more recent years, some Arab Christian ministries have been added as well. Jill also leads tours to Israel and coordinates the Israel 24/7 prayer wall.

Jill has also written, *The Anzac Call* which outlines the significant part the ANZACs (Australian and New Zealand Army Corps) played in the Middle East in WW1, and connects this to the end-time prophecies of the Bible. It also calls for the raising up of the spiritual Anzac army, and calls the church and nation to stand with Israel today.
watchmen777@optusnet.com.au

To the Glory of God

For His eternal faithfulness

to His covenant promises

to Israel and His church

and for His invitation for us

to participate in their outworking today

Contents

Acknowledgements 1

Foreword 3

Introduction

Welcome 5

The Parable of the Fig Tree 7

God's Prophetic Plan of Redemption 15

Re-aligning to God's Prophetic Timing 23

The Feasts of the Lord: God's Appointed Times 27

       Their Prophetic Importance 33

Feast Dates 2020-2030 37

The Monthly Prayer Focus

January – Israel's Glorious Destiny 43

       Why Pray for the Jewish People and Israel? 46

February – Seeds of Faith – Congregations in the Land 57

March – Preservation and Return – Aliya; Festival of Purim 73

April – First Fruits of Redemption – Spring Feast Period 83

May – Rebirth of a Nation – Israel's Modern Beginnings;

       Government; Feast of Shavuot 93

June – Defending God's Purposes – Survival of the Nation; the IDF   105

July – Clearing the Stones – Anti-Semitism and Replacement Theology   119

August – Removing the Veil – Judaism; Jewish Denominations 133

September – Opening a Cleansing Fountain – Fall Feast Period 145

October – Prophesying Life to the Dry Bones – Day to Pray;

    Ministries in the Land 161

November – Grafted in to the Olive Tree

    Gentiles Sharing with Israel 177

December – A House of Prayer for all Nations

    Festival of Hanukka; Nations Aligning with Israel 187

Appendix 1 – Relating to Jewish People 201

Appendix 2 – Testimonies 209

Appendix 3 – Synagogue Readings for the High Holy Days 221

Appendix 4 – Resources 223

International Coordinators 227

Other Materials by the Same Author 229

Donation Details 230

Gifts for the King 231

Acknowledgements

My great appreciation goes to the ministry leaders and pastors, Jewish and Arab, who have responded and contributed over the last 18 years, some many times as their ministries have grown.

I am greatly indebted to my formatter who, despite working full time and more, finds the time to make the production look professional and administer the website. My pastor Graham Holman has faithfully supported this ministry since its inception and assists in the area of banking, finance and oversight. My thanks also go to Rabbi Lawrence Hirsch who has given guidance from a Messianic perspective, ministry support and also willingly shared his excellent photographic talents. Susan Pierotti generously gives of her time and professional skills for editing, while Gerredina Kovac and Eulalie Holman have also helped with proofreading. Thank you to Jenny Hagger, Lawrence Hirsch, Rick Ridings and Bishop Robert Stearns for their kind words of endorsement.

The international coordinators have assisted for many years to gather the intercessors in their nations to pray with us for the Jewish people, and print and distribute the booklets. May God bless you for your support.

Over the years, through your purchases and donations we have been able to support Jewish ministries (and of late some Arab ones also) with over $160,000 as well as your prayer support. We are happy to continue to forward donations and profits to the ministries. We donate this directly to the bank accounts of the congregations and ministries in the Jewish and Israel Prayer Focus, many of which we visit during our tours. You can donate over the web at http://jewishandisraelprayerfocus.org.

Most important of all, I want to thank you, our faithful intercessors for God's people, without whom the ministry would have no point. God hears your prayers and sends His ministering angels in answer to them. May you see the fullness of your hidden service. God bless you as you pray for the peace of Jerusalem (Ps 122:6) and the salvation of all Israel (Rom 11:26).

Every effort has been made to contact those who have written or approved the articles republished in this book. If the email has been incorrect or I have not received a reply, I have assumed that the original approval given for the JPF publication is sufficient to reprint. Likewise, all photos from the congregations have been originally supplied for the JPF with previous years' articles.

Photos credits: All portrait photos in the articles are supplied by the writers. Photos in the book are from Jill Curry's private collection, except those which are courtesy of Lawrence Hirsch, the Introduction Facing Page by David Nesher, and the following which come from the web:

March 1. Jews returning to Israel https://commons.wikimedia.org/wiki Category:Immigrants_to_Israel#/media/File:December_Charter_Flight.jpg

2. Esther scroll https://commons.wikimedia.org/wiki/File:Esther_Scroll_-_Google_Art_Project.jpg

May 1. Beersheba charge: Australian War Memorial – Disputed picture of the charge at Beersheba (or re-enactment), https://www.awm.gov.au/collection/A02684

2. Palestinian Mandate. Map of Partition of Palestine – https://commons.wikimedia.org/wiki/File:PalestineAndTransjordan.png – Doron

June 1. Rabbi Goren blows the shofar at the Western Wall in 1967 just after the capture. By Government Press Office (Israel), CC BY-SA 4.0, https://commons.wikimedia.org/w/index.php?curid=59598328

2. By Israel Defense Forces - IDF Soldiers at the Western Wall, CC BY-SA 2.0, https://commons.wikimedia.org/w/index.php?curid=34369288

Foreword

There is a growing hunger amongst Israelis to know the truth about the Messiah. While certain elements staunchly resist anything to do with Yeshua/Jesus (or Yeshu – a derogatory term), largely because of historical abuse and persecution by Christians, there are 42,000 Israelis subscribed to watch Hebrew language videos produced by 'One for Israel', a Messianic evangelistic organisation! God is moving, congregations are growing and multiplying, and many Arabic and Jewish believers are coming together as one in Christ. You will not hear this on the normal news channels, which rarely report any good news, let alone from Israel, but one purpose of this book is to give insight into what God is doing amongst His people and to encourage you to join with Him to bring the people and the nation into its glorious destiny.

This year sees a substantial change in the form of the Jewish and Israel Prayer Focus. Instead of the usual 22 days of prayer only for the High Holy Days season, we are moving to an annual format and providing you with website links for you to personally connect with the congregations and ministries that most touch your hearts. An annual booklet will no longer be produced but the bi-monthly newsletter will continue, as will the alternate monthly prayer letter, for which you are encouraged to sign up.
Contact: watchmen777@optusnet.com.au

This book is not meant to be read all at once. It is a handbook and prayer guide for daily prayer 365 days a year or perhaps in small groups. There is teaching material each month, followed by daily prayer points at the end. It is hoped that it will spark interest which can be further pursued by making contact with the congregations and ministries or by joining the Jewish and Israel Prayer Focus Newsletter and Prayer Letter for ongoing prayer updates.

Note:
The name of Jesus in Hebrew is Yeshua, meaning salvation, so this title is often used in this book. Some Jewish writers also use 'YHVH' or 'G_d' or 'HaShem' for God's name in the tradition of not writing or speaking the holy name of God.

Welcome

As I write this, the world is reeling with the COVID-19 coronavirus pandemic. People all across the globe are undergoing enforced restrictions limiting movement, there are millions of casualties, untold numbers are losing their jobs, businesses are going under, hundreds of thousands have died, and life is anything but normal. Only a couple of months ago, had someone told us that 2020 would begin like this, we could not have imagined such a scenario in our wildest nightmare. This tsunami of sickness and death has suddenly erupted and changed life as we once knew it. What was formally movie fiction is now reality. The world is at war with an unseen enemy that is wreaking havoc from the halls of parliaments to the gutters in almost every nation, rich and poor.

Such a violent global shaking should not surprise those who have read what the Scriptures say about the end times. Jesus warned us of 'birth pangs' that would come upon the world that would usher in a time of tribulation leading to His return and the coming kingdom.

For nation will rise against nation, and kingdom against kingdom, and in various places there will be famines and earthquakes. But all these things are the beginning of birth pangs. Matt 24:7-8.

We saw nations at war in WWI and WWII but those of us fortunate enough to live in the Western nations have lived in peace for a full generation. That has now abruptly changed. This biological catastrophe has surely advanced the one-world-government agenda in leaps and bounds. Never have we known such restrictions on our freedom – though others in non-Western nations have suffered horrendous persecution in that time. The cashless society has rocketed forward and online trading is now the new necessity. The world will never be the same again.

When birth pangs begin they are unstoppable and increase in frequency and severity until the birth. We can expect a rocky road in the days ahead but there is a glorious future awaiting those who know and trust in the Lord Jesus Christ.

In 2019, the Lord told me to 'gather up the last 18 years of the *Jewish Prayer Focus* and put it into a larger prayer book that will provide a prayer guide for a whole year, not just the 22 days of the biblical High Holy Days in September-October'. So in obedience, here it is!

As per the original vision of the *Jewish Prayer Focus,* it will provide insight into Jewish thought and practice from biblical and current times, give links to congregations and ministries in Israel, supply prayer points and a list of resources. Its aim is to help Christians worldwide to understand the connection between the prophecies of the Bible and what God is doing with His Jewish brethren today, including those yet to be fulfilled, and equip them to pray for the *restoration of all things about which God spoke by the mouth of His holy prophets from ancient time* (Acts 3:21), which Peter said must happen before Jesus will return from Heaven. We will take note of the sign of the fig tree as it puts forth its leaves and be doing as Jesus told us – standing in the day of battle, looking up as His redemption draws nigh, watching and praying and preparing the way for His return as King (Lk 21:28-36).

The Parable of the Fig Tree

We serve a God who is faithful. He is not a god of our imagination based on the fickle character of humans, like the Greek gods. He is not subject to the wiles of man but is sovereign and totally dependable. When we see how God has fulfilled so many Scriptures in such detail through the birth, life, death and resurrection of Jesus, we can have complete confidence that the Scriptures referring to Jesus' coming as king will also be fulfilled. Despite the fact that the world is getting darker and more uncertain, as we study His Word, focus on our beautiful, risen Lord and remind the Father of what He has said, we can be excited about what is to come.

Then they will see the Son of Man coming in a cloud with power and great glory. But when these things begin to take place, straighten up and lift up your heads, because your redemption is drawing near." Lk 21:27-28

Primary Scriptures Concerning Jesus' Return

The Scriptures referring to the Messiah coming as a suffering servant in His priestly role have been fulfilled. His life, death, resurrection and ascension have been completed and the victory over death has been won. Our salvation is through His completed work alone and we cannot attain it by human effort or good works. We no longer need a sacrificial system since Jesus' blood has been shed for our sin. 'It is finished' and can never be repeated, replaced or cancelled. So what Scriptures have not been fulfilled? The Scriptures referring to Jesus' coming as king on earth have not yet come to pass. These are glorious Scriptures.

But immediately after the tribulation of those days the sun will be darkened, and the moon will not give its light, and the stars will fall from the sky, and the powers of the heavens will be shaken. And then the sign of the Son of Man will appear in the sky, and then all the tribes of the earth will mourn, and they will see the Son of Man coming on the clouds of the sky with power and great glory. And He will send forth His angels with a great trumpet and they will gather together His elect from the four winds, from one end of the sky to the other. Matt 24:29-31

In this passage from the Olivet sermon, Jesus refers to the book of Daniel and the vision he saw of the coming of the Son of Man to receive His kingdom on earth.

I kept looking in the night visions, and behold, with the clouds of heaven One like a Son of Man was coming, and He came up to the Ancient of Days and was presented before Him. And to Him was given dominion, glory and a kingdom that all the peoples, nations and men of every language might serve Him. His dominion is an everlasting dominion which will not pass away; and His kingdom is one which will not be destroyed. Dan 7:13-14

The apostle John saw Jesus' return, riding on a white horse.

And I saw heaven opened, and behold, a white horse, and He who sat on it is called Faithful and True, and in righteousness He judges and wages war. His eyes are a flame of fire, and on His head are many diadems; and He has a name written on Him which no one knows except Himself. He is clothed with a robe dipped in blood, and His name is called The Word of God. And the armies which are in heaven, clothed in fine linen, white and clean, were following Him on white horses. From His mouth comes a sharp sword, so that with it He may strike down the nations, and He will rule them with a rod of iron; and He treads the wine press of the fierce wrath of God, the Almighty. And on His robe and on His thigh He has a name written, "King of kings and Lord of lords." Rev 19:11-16

End-time Signs

Towards the end of His life on earth, Jesus taught the disciples about the end-times and the signs of His coming. He warned of times of tribulation and that they should flee Jerusalem when it was surrounded by armies (Lk 21:20-22). This is an impossible thing to do! However, His words came true when the siege of Jerusalem was broken for 18 months by the death of the Emperor Nero in mid-68 CE and the ensuing instability that followed as various ones vied for the leadership, until Vespasian came to the throne at the end of 69 CE. This gave the disciples time to flee before the destruction of the city and temple in August 70 CE.

The Sign of the Fig Tree

Following this, He said there would be signs in the sun and moon and a shaking of the heavens (Lk 21:25-27), then the Son of Man would be seen as clearly as lightning as He came on the clouds with power and great glory (Matt 24:27-31). He gave them the parable of the fig tree, as the sign of the last days (Matt 24:32-34, Lk 21:29-31). The fig tree, along with the vine, is a symbol for Israel (1 Kg 4:25, Zech 3:10). Both are part of the seven species of the land (Deut 8:8). Jesus had spoken to the unfruitful fig tree a few days before (Matt 21:18-19) and it had withered as a sign that the nation would be unfruitful, but He said now that it would once again bear leaves and is the sign of the end-time events that would herald His soon-coming. The shooting fig leaves are a symbol for the Jewish return and life returning to the land. When we see that happening, we can know that 'He is near'. We live in these exciting days and the return of the Jews and establishment of the nation of Israel is that sign.

Now learn the parable from the fig tree: when its branch has already become tender and puts forth its leaves, you know that summer is near; so, you too, when you see all these things, recognize that He is near, right at the door. Matt 24:32-33

Establishing His Throne on Earth

Jesus said quite clearly that He would return to earth, not just meet us departing to be with Him in Heaven. He taught His disciples to pray 'Your Kingdom come; Your will be done on earth as it is in Heaven' (Matt 6:10). He will return to the Mount of Olives (Zech 14:4, Acts 1:11-12) which will split in two, and will take His place on the throne in Jerusalem (Zech 14:9) and rule the nations with righteousness (Rev 19:15, Is 2:1-4, 9:7, Ps 2, Ps 97:1-2).

For I will gather all the nations against Jerusalem to battle, and the city will be captured, the houses plundered, the women ravished and half of the city exiled, but the rest of the people will not be cut off from the city. Then the LORD will go forth and fight against those nations, as when He fights on a day of battle. In that day His feet will stand on the Mount of Olives, which is in front of Jerusalem on the east; and the Mount of Olives will be split in its middle from east to west by a very large valley, so that half of the mountain will move toward the north and the other half toward the south. You will flee by the valley of My mountains, for the valley of the mountains will reach to Azel; yes, you will flee just as you fled before the earthquake in the days of Uzziah king of Judah. Then the LORD, my God, will come, and all the holy ones with Him! Zech 14:2-5

And the LORD will be king over all the earth; in that day the LORD will be the only one, and His name the only one. Zech 14:9

It appears from this passage in Zechariah that His coming is associated with a forced evacuation of Jews from half of Jerusalem in a time of great tribulation as the nations assemble to come against Jerusalem to divide it. Hmm...that sounds rather familiar, does it not? The agenda of the United Nations is very anti-Israel and the status of Jerusalem is the biggest sticking point. Zechariah again predicted this:

Behold, I am going to make Jerusalem a cup that causes reeling to all the peoples around; and when the siege is against Jerusalem, it will also be against Judah. It will come about in that day that I will make Jerusalem a heavy stone for all the peoples; all who lift it will be severely injured. And all the nations of the earth will be gathered against it. Zech 12:2-3

The reason that Jerusalem is so controversial is because it is to be the throne of the King of kings and Satan wants that throne.

Why are the nations in an uproar and the peoples devising a vain thing? The kings of the earth take their stand and the rulers take counsel together against the LORD and against His Anointed, saying, "Let us tear their fetters apart and cast away their cords from us!" He who sits in the heavens laughs, the Lord scoffs at them. Then He will speak to them in His anger and terrify them in His fury, saying, "But as for Me, I have installed My King upon Zion, My holy mountain." I will surely tell of the decree of the LORD: He said to Me, "You are My Son, Today I have begotten You." Ps 2:1-7

Preparing for His Coming

There are certain things which must take place before Jesus will return.

1. The gospel must go to all people

This gospel of the kingdom shall be preached in the whole world as a testimony to all the nations, and then the end will come. Matt 24:14

2. The Bride of Christ must make herself ready

Let us rejoice and be glad and give the glory to Him, for the marriage of the Lamb has come and His bride has made herself ready. It was given to her to clothe herself in fine linen, bright and clean; for the fine linen is the righteous acts of the saints. Rev 19:7-8

3. The Jewish people must welcome Him

Behold, your house is being left to you desolate! For I say to you, from now on you will not see Me until you say, 'Blessed is He who comes in the name of the Lord!'" Matt 23:39

This Messianic greeting is the Hebrew way of saying 'Welcome'.

4. The Restoration of all things about which the prophets prophesied must happen

But the things which God announced beforehand by the mouth of all the prophets, that His Christ would suffer, He has thus fulfilled. Therefore repent and return, so that your sins may be wiped away, in order that times of refreshing may come from the presence of the Lord; and that He may send Jesus, the Christ appointed for you, whom heaven must receive until the period of restoration of all things about which God spoke by the mouth of His holy prophets from ancient time. Acts 3:18-21

5. The times of the Gentiles must come to an end

They will fall by the sword and will be taken as prisoners to all the nations. Jerusalem will be trampled on by the Gentiles until the times of the Gentiles are fulfilled. Lk 21:24

The first two of these points refer to the church and the second three are more aligned with the Jews. While the church is aware of the great commission of Jesus (even if it has not carried it out very well on the whole), and at least some are seeking to live purified lives, the place of the Jewish people in this preparation has been largely ignored by the broader church. A small remnant in the church is waking up to this and standing with Israel, more so in the US than elsewhere. Gentile nations have ruled Jerusalem for 2,000 years since 70 CE but since the late 19th century the fig tree has begun to shoot forth its leaves. In 1967, Israel regained control of Jerusalem in a war forced upon them in which they had no intention of taking the city. It is important for intercessors to understand this key concept and pray for the wider church to catch God's purposes.

Connecting to Prophetic Destiny

Prophetic destiny is the future that has been foretold by God through His prophets. The clearest examples of this are where He established His covenants, as we know that God is trustworthy and will not change His character or break His covenantal promises.

We connect to prophetic destiny by agreeing with it and praying into being what the Scriptures have said will be fulfilled. We are not praying our own ideas or desires. We are reminding God of His Word and His covenants. As such, we are joining with Heaven, preparing the way for the coming of the Messiah and becoming part of the answer. We cannot go wrong with that kind of prayer.

Praying Prophetically

Prophetic prayer is not the same as reacting to what is happening in the physical realm. It is not the same as praying for a political entity. It is seeing God's purposes from the Scriptures and praying into being the words of the prophets, thus entering the spiritual realm and praying together with Jesus. We are to support God's kingdom work, not a country or even a particular people group, even though the restoration of the nation of Israel is part of God's plan. We need to be discerning, not be caught up in thinking Israel is perfect. The salvation of the people and the bringing forth of the nation into its biblical destiny are to be our focus.

Many Christians, albeit mostly unwittingly, are supporting religious Judaism at the expense of the Messianic Jews and Arab Christians who take the gospel to their people. Many of the large Jewish organisations are picking up on the Christian interest in Israel and enticing Christians to support their work. Most of these are worthy humanitarian causes and certainly not bad, but why is so much Christian money, especially from the US, not aiding our own brothers and sisters in the Land who are often doing the same humanitarian work? Is it not time we connected with our own brethren, stood with them and furthered the cause of the gospel? It is true that the history of Christian persecution of the Jews (see July) has left a very sour taste in the mouths of most Jews and can only be removed by a pure witness of unconditional love. Thus, our support for all Jews, whether believers or not at this stage, is needed. However, I believe that our primary calling is to support God's kingdom purposes through the 'first fruits' believers.

God's Prophetic Plan of Redemption

God's Prophetic Purposes for the Jewish People

God has a big plan that He unfolded through the Scriptures from Genesis to Revelation for the redemption of individuals and the redemption of nations. Genesis chapter 3 outlines the fall of man and promise of redemption through the seed of a woman. In Genesis chapters 10-11, the nations were trying to become God and God scattered them, confusing their language. In the next chapter, He gives us the key to the redemption of the nations through one obedient man, Abraham and His descendents, who became the nation of Israel. The LORD had said to Abram:

Go from your country, your people and your father's household to the land I will show you. I will make you into a great nation, and I will bless you; I will make your name great, and you will be a blessing. I will bless those who bless you, and whoever curses you I will curse; and all peoples on earth will be blessed through you. Gen 12:1-3 (NIV)

God established an everlasting covenant with Abraham and His descendents and gave them a homeland as an eternal possession.

I will establish my covenant as an everlasting covenant between me [God] and you [Abraham] and your descendants after you for the generations to come, to be your God and the God of your descendants after you. The whole land of Canaan, where you now reside as a foreigner, I will give as an everlasting possession to you and your descendants after you; and I will be their God. Gen 17:7-8 (NIV)

God knew this nation would reject Him, fall into idolatry and be cast out of their land as punishment but He also promised a return. Their disobedience and subsequent exile was prophesied in Deuteronomy chapters 29-30 so it was no surprise to God. Despite their disobedience His covenant love remained, as did His covenant promise to restore the people from the ends of the earth a second time to their homeland in the end times.

In that day the Lord will reach out his hand a second time to reclaim the surviving remnant of his people from Assyria, from Lower Egypt, from Upper Egypt, from Cush, from Elam, from Babylonia, from Hamath and from the islands of the Mediterranean. He will raise a banner for the nations and gather the exiles of Israel; he will assemble the scattered people of Judah from the four quarters of the earth. Isaiah 11:11-12 (NIV)

In Ezekiel chapters 35-37, the prophet talks about Edom (part of today's Jordan) and the nations that reside around Israel that scorn His people and want to possess their land. He says He will act to judge them out of His jealousy and for the sake of His name. He sets out a long list of 'I wills' in response to the actions of the nations that come against His people.

And you, son of man, prophesy to the mountains of Israel and say, 'O mountains of Israel, hear the word of the LORD. Thus says the Lord GOD, "Because the enemy has spoken against you, 'Aha!' and, 'The everlasting heights have become our possession,' therefore prophesy and say, 'Thus says the Lord GOD, "For good reason they have made you desolate and crushed you from every side, that you would become a possession of the rest of the nations and you have been taken up in the talk and the whispering of the people."' Therefore, O mountains of Israel, hear the word of the Lord GOD. Thus says the Lord GOD to the mountains and to the hills, to the ravines and to the valleys, to the desolate wastes and to the forsaken cities which have become a prey and a derision to the rest of the nations which are round about, therefore thus says the Lord GOD, "Surely in the fire of My jealousy I have spoken against the rest of the nations, and against all Edom, who appropriated My land for themselves as a possession with wholehearted joy and with scorn of soul, to drive it out for a prey." Therefore prophesy concerning the land of Israel and say to the mountains and to the hills, to the ravines and to the valleys, "Thus says the Lord GOD, 'Behold, I have spoken in My jealousy and in My wrath because you have endured the insults of the nations.' Therefore thus says the Lord GOD, 'I have sworn that surely the nations which are around you will themselves endure their insults. But you, O mountains of Israel, you will put forth your branches and bear your fruit for My people Israel; for they will soon come. For, behold, I am for you, and I will turn to you, and you will be cultivated and sown. I will multiply men on you, all the house of Israel, all of it; and the cities will be inhabited and the waste places will be rebuilt. I will multiply on you man and beast; and they will increase and be fruitful; and I will cause you to be inhabited as you were formerly and will treat you better than at the first. Thus you will know that I am the LORD. Yes, I will cause men—My people Israel—to walk on you and possess you, so that you will become their inheritance and never again bereave them of children.' Ezek 36:1-12

Therefore say to the Israelites, 'This is what the Sovereign LORD says: It is not for your sake, people of Israel, that I am going to do these things, but for the sake of my holy name, which you have profaned among the nations where you have gone. I will show the holiness of my great name...Then the nations will know that I am the LORD, declares the Sovereign LORD, when I am proved holy through you before their eyes.'

'For I will take you out of the nations; I will gather you from all the countries and bring you back into your own land. I will sprinkle clean water on you, and you will be clean; I will cleanse you from all your impurities and from all your idols. I will give you a new heart and put a new spirit in you; I will remove from you your heart of stone and give you a heart of flesh. And I will put my Spirit in you and move you to follow my decrees and be careful to keep my laws. Then you will live in the land I gave your ancestors; you will be my people, and I will be your God. Ezekiel 36:22-28 (NIV)

Jeremiah chapters 30-31 outline much the same pattern and it concludes with this promise.

"The days are coming," declares the LORD, "when I will make a new covenant with the people of Israel and with the people of Judah... "I will put my law in their minds and write it on their hearts. I will be their God, and they will be my people ... they will all know me, from the least of them to the greatest," declares the LORD. "For I will forgive their wickedness and will remember their sins no more." This is what the LORD says, he who appoints the sun to shine by day, who decrees the moon and stars to shine by

night, who stirs up the sea so that its waves roar— the LORD Almighty is his name: "Only if these decrees vanish from my sight," declares the LORD, "will Israel ever cease being a nation before me." Jer 31:31-37 (NIV)

We see a general pattern of restoration and order of events here:

- a regathering of the scattered people from the ends of the earth back to their land
- restoration of the productivity of the land
- restoration of the nation
- rebuilding of cities
- cleansing and revival of hearts
- a new covenant relationship

While these promises were written to Israel before the return from Babylon, they were only fulfilled in part as the people were not scattered to the ends of the earth and their spiritual renewal was also only minimally begun. However, we can see that this restoration is unfolding in our day and is well underway already. Still there is more to come and we are invited to join with the Lord to see the fulfilment completed.

We need to now look at the New Testament for further clarification of God's purposes for the Jews and how the Gentiles fit into the picture.

How God Wants Jews and Gentiles to Function Together for His Glory

Romans chapters 9-11 are key to the understanding of God's end-time purposes. Paul wrote to the Romans to answer a number of questions they had, one of which was 'Has God finished with the Jews?' or in other words, 'Is the church now the new Israel?' Emperor Claudius had evicted 40,000 Jews from Rome in 49 CE, two of whom, Aquila and his wife Priscilla, moved to Corinth (Acts 18:2). Claudius died in 54 BC after which his successor, Nero, invited them back. In the absence of the Jews, Gentile Christians would have to lead the church. On the Jews' return, who should now lead – Jew or Gentile – was a burning question. Paul addresses this in Romans chapters 9-11.

In chapter 9, he argues that God's calling establishes who belong to Him – the promise was through Isaac, not Ishmael, and that God calls some Gentiles who were not His people 'My people'. Righteousness is attained by faith, not works. In chapter 10, he expands the concept of righteousness. It does not come through the law but through calling on God and belief in Jesus. This applies to both Jews and Gentiles without distinction. But they need to hear the gospel in order to choose.

Grafted in to the Olive Tree

Chapter 11 begins:

I ask then: Did God reject his people? By no means! I am an Israelite myself, a descendant of Abraham, from the tribe of Benjamin. God did not reject his people, whom he foreknew. Rom 11:1-2a (NIV)

So Paul is absolutely clear that God has not finished with the Jews. He gives us another part of God's big plan for the salvation of the nations – the heart of the Jews has been hardened for a time so that the Gentile nations would hear the gospel. Their salvation would make the Jews jealous so that they would then have their eyes opened and the Jewish nation would again find their salvation. Paul breaks into praise at the unfathomable wisdom of God's plan.

Again I ask: Did they stumble so as to fall beyond recovery? Not at all! Rather, because of their transgression, salvation has come to the Gentiles to make Israel envious. But if their transgression means riches for the world, and their loss means riches for the Gentiles, how much greater riches will their full inclusion bring!

I am talking to you Gentiles. Inasmuch

as I am the apostle to the Gentiles, I take pride in my ministry in the hope that I may somehow arouse my own people to envy and save some of them. For if their rejection brought reconciliation to the world, what will their acceptance be but life from the dead?...

If some of the branches have been broken off, and you, though a wild olive shoot, have been grafted in among the others and now share in the nourishing sap from the olive root, do not consider yourself to be superior to those other branches. If you do, consider this: You do not support the root, but the root supports you. You will say then, "Branches were broken off so that I could be grafted in." Granted. But they were broken off because of unbelief, and you stand by faith. Do not be arrogant, but tremble. For if God did not spare the natural branches, he will not spare you either.

Consider therefore the kindness and sternness of God: sternness to those who fell, but kindness to you, provided that you continue in his kindness. Otherwise, you also will be cut off. And if they do not persist in unbelief, they will be grafted in, for God is able to graft them in again. After all, if you were cut out of an olive tree that is wild by nature, and contrary to nature were grafted into a cultivated olive tree, how much more readily will these, the natural branches, be grafted into their own olive tree!

I do not want you to be ignorant of this mystery, brothers and sisters, so that you may not be conceited: Israel has experienced a hardening in part until the full number of the Gentiles has come in, and in this way all Israel will be saved. Rom 11:11-26a (NIV)

One New Man in Christ

Paul teaches us that Jews and Gentiles are to be grafted in to the same olive tree. The Jewish unbelief is for a time and that at the end of the times of the Gentiles, the full harvest will come in and all Israel will be saved. In his letter to the Ephesians, he calls this new entity of Jew and Gentile 'one new man'.

But now in Christ Jesus you who formerly were far off have been brought near by the blood of Christ. For He Himself is our peace, who made both groups into one and broke down the barrier of the dividing wall, by abolishing in His flesh the enmity, which is the Law of commandments contained in ordinances, so that in Himself He might make the two into one new man, thus establishing peace, and might reconcile them both in one body to God through the cross, by it having put to death the enmity. Eph 2:13-16

So God's plan is not to have two brides or even separate streams that reject each other but that the two may become one in Him.

Redemption of the Nations

Not only does God have an individual plan of redemption but also a global plan for the nations. Israel is the key to the redemption of the nations as their salvation will bring *life from the dead* (revival) – Rom 11:15. God has not forgotten the Gentiles as His plan involves a highway of blessing from the Nile to the Euphrates and beyond. These rivers of blessing will flow to the ends of the earth. What a glorious day that will be.

In that day there will be a highway from Egypt to Assyria, and the Assyrians will come into Egypt and the Egyptians into Assyria, and the Egyptians will worship with the Assyrians. In that day Israel will be the third party with Egypt and Assyria, a blessing in the midst of the earth, whom the LORD of hosts has blessed, saying, "Blessed is Egypt My people, and Assyria the work of My hands, and Israel My inheritance." Isaiah 19:23-25

Re-Aligning to God's Prophetic Timing

Those called to pray prophetically need to learn to align not only with God's will but also with God's timing. This is crucial as God is working on His own calendar not a man-made one.

The Gregorian calendar, which the Western world uses today to calculate time and dates, stems from the time of Pope Gregory XIII (1502-1585). Prior to that, the Julian calendar, introduced by Julius Caesar in 45 BCE, was in use. In this Roman calendar, days begin at midnight, weeks begin at midnight on Saturday-Sunday and many of the months are named after Roman and Norse gods.

In contrast, God gave us His calculation at the creation of time in the Garden of Eden. Biblical days begin at sundown, weeks begin after the Sabbath ends on Saturday evening, and months are based on a lunar cycle, beginning when the first sliver of the moon is sighted in the sky by two priestly witnesses in Jerusalem. Years were 12 or 13 months long (called a leap month), depending on the ripening of the barley harvest at the beginning of the first month, called Aviv or Nisan. If the barley was not sufficiently ripe, an extra month was added. The two witnesses, heaven (moon) and earth (barley), worked together to announce the new biblical year.

The yearly cycle was set with appointed times in the form of the Biblical Feasts, which begin with the spring feasts of Passover (Pesach), Unleavened  Bread and First Fruits, then 50 days later, Pentecost (Shavuot). In the autumn are the latter feasts of Trumpets (Yom HaTruah), the Day of Atonement (Yom Kippur) and Tabernacles (Sukkot). There were also the 7-year cycles of the Sabbath Year and, after 7x7 yearly cycles, the 50th year celebration of the Jubilee Year.

For the first 350 years after Christ this reckoning continued, even in exile. Once the new moon was seen in Jerusalem, fires were lit on hilltops all the way to Babylon. In 359 CE the rabbis changed this reckoning and adopted an astronomical calculation, where a leap year was inserted seven of every 19 years, irrespective of the state of the crops in Israel. This calculation is still used in most of Judaism today.

However, God is restoring all things. Nehemia Gordon, determined to resurrect the ancient method of calculation, researched this for over a decade. He is now Israel's foremost authority on the subject. The exciting news is that since the year 2000, the ancient method is again being calculated. It has now been observed indisputably that the rabbinic astronomical calendar is often incorrect. You can find more at https://karaite-korner.org.

The only one of the annual biblical feasts that occurs at the beginning of the month is the Feast of Trumpets. Everyone knew approximately when it would occur, but not the exact time. One had to wait until the moon was sighted by two or three priestly witnesses before celebrating the holiday. Thus the Feast of Trumpets became known as the Feast where 'no one knows the day or hour' of its occurrence. This has obvious implications for Jesus' teachings about the day and hour of His return.

As we will see, God is working on His calendar calculations, since He fulfilled all the spring feasts according to His biblical calendar. Even in recent times, there is evidence He is continuing to do so. Had this harvest calculation been used in 1948, the State of Israel may well have been born at Pentecost! The seven-year Oslo covenant was ratified on the Feast of Trumpets in 1993, and annulled seven years later on the Feast of Trumpets, when Ariel (meaning 'lion of God') Sharon went up onto Temple Mount and read the prophecy from Ezekiel about the reunification of Israel and Judah. The violence that followed ensured the 'covenant with death' was annulled. The first stock-market crash in the US in 2001 occurred on the 29th day of Elul, the exact day on the Hebrew calendar when in the 7th 'Shmittah' (Sabbath) year, debts were to be released. Seven years later on the 29th day of Elul,

2008, once again the stock market crashed!

Messianic Rabbi Jonathan Cahn notes that the beginning of the end-time restoration of the Jews is tied to the proclamation of a foreigner who comes to the land and witnesses the devastation which has resulted from the curse (Deut 29:22-29). Mark Twain (aka Samuel Langhorne Clemens) visited the Holy Land in 1867 and wrote about what he saw in his book, *The Innocents Abroad*. Fifty years (Jubilee) later was the liberation of Beersheba by the British and ANZAC forces and the declaration of the Balfour Declaration, both on the same day, 31st October, 1917, which opened the way physically and politically for the Jews to return. Another 50 years on, in 1967, Jerusalem was dramatically re-united under Israeli control. In 2017, in the next Jubilee year, President Trump moved the US Embassy to Jerusalem, declaring it the capital of Israel.

Not only do the events coincide with biblical festivals and dates but, as Rabbi Cahn points out, time and time again the Sabbath readings for these events were prophetically related to what occurred. You can find a list of Rabbi Cahn's books in the resources section at the end of this book or for a first taste, have a look at Sid Roth's interview with Jonathan Cahn https://www.youtube.com/watch?v=ieIIakmwFy8 about his book, *The Oracle: Ancient Prophecy Foretelling Trump & End Times*.

It appears that the Creator is still running His universe according to His time clock, and it is the church that does not understand the signs because it is not aligned with His calendar. The sleeping church does not know the season of Christ's return: the prophetically alert 'ekklesia', who know and practise God's appointed calendar will recognise the nearness of His return.

Will we be bold enough to step beyond our traditions and walk into alignment with God's appointment calendar, timing, plans for the universe, and appointed times, when He desires His family to meet at His table and partake of His feasts?

The Feasts of the Lord

And God said, "Let there be lights in the vault of the sky to separate the day from the night, and let them serve as signs to mark sacred times, and days and years. Genesis 1:14 (NIV)

The word used in the NIV for 'sacred times' or in the NASB 'seasons' is the Hebrew word 'mo'ed' or plural 'mo'edim'; meaning appointed time/s. God has an appointment calendar where He set dates on which He wanted the Hebrew people to meet with Him to remember Him and what He has done. God calls these festivals '*My* appointed times' and the 'Feasts of the *Lord*', not the feasts of the Jews (Lev 23:2,4). The same word in Hebrew also means a dress rehearsal. So what are these feasts a rehearsal for? We shall see shortly.

Every nation has festivals to commemorate important events in their history and religious festivals to remember their roots. It is the most powerful way to pass on this history to our children. Israel does too but some of these were not appointed by man but by God Himself. God told the people to celebrate Passover annually to remember the Exodus (Ex 12:14-17). Purim was instituted to remember the deliverance from Haman's evil plan of annihilation in Persia, which Queen Esther interceded to stop (Esther 9:20-21, 30-32).

The Feast Calendar

The Appointed Times of the Lord begin with the Sabbath (Lev 23:1-3), which is a weekly celebration, not a yearly one. Based on God's example of resting on the seventh day, Shabbat was given before Sinai and sanctified by God Himself (Gen 2:2). It was to be remembered and observed (Ex 20:8-11, Deut 5:12-15), and was a sign and a covenant between God and

Photo Lawrence Hirsch

His people (Ex 31:12-17). No normal work was to be done but Jesus declared that healing, doing good and saving life were priorities. He is Lord of the Sabbath (Matt 12:8) and He said that the Sabbath was made for man, not man for the Sabbath (Mk 2:27-28). There are special blessings for Gentiles who keep the Sabbath (Is 56:2-7, 58:13-14) and in the New Testament there is also a Sabbath rest for the people of God (Heb 4:9-10).

Shabbat – Jill Shannon 2019

Shabbat was not first introduced as part of the Mosaic Covenant. It was introduced several thousand years before Moses at the creation of the world – long before there were any Jews on the earth! God ceased His work on the seventh day in order to spend time in fellowship with Adam and Eve on their first day on earth, thus setting it aside as holy (Gen 2:2-3, Ex 20:11). This surely must mean that God meant it for everyone, not just for the Jewish people. In Exodus 20:8-10 the servants, the foreigners and even the animals were to take a day's break! Here again we see God's inclusion of the Gentiles in the holy day of rest.

There are two words for rest in Hebrew – the first is *manoach* which means to rest because you are tired, such as the dove in Genesis 8:9. This is also the root of Noah's name. The other is Shabbat which is to stop normal activity. God was not tired from His work of creation but He did cease His activity.

In our stressful lives, filled with so many demands on our time, it would seem that people would be only too happy to stop and enjoy the Sabbath rest, but it appears that just as the Israelites in the desert still tried to gather manna or wood on the day of rest, so we also find the fourth commandment one of the hardest to keep. The Sabbath is meant to be a blessing to humanity, not bondage, so why do we find it so difficult? All relationships require time spent together to nurture and develop. Are we simply distracted or are we really afraid of intimacy with the Lord?

Perhaps we just need to manage our time better, or perhaps work has become an idol and time has become such a precious commodity that we cannot 'afford' to 'waste' it by spending it with the Lord. Mary is remembered because she 'wasted' the precious oil on Jesus' feet (Jn 12:1-8). A deep reward is assured for those who would linger in His presence. It can take time to be able to unwind and hear the voice of God but it is infinitely worth brushing aside the clutter to come into the throne room of Almighty God, minister our love to Him and allow Him to minister His love to our deepest needs and equip us to take that love to others. The Sabbath is dear to the Lord. May it be dear to our hearts also.

Insights from Jill Shannon's book A Prophetic Calendar – the Feasts of Israel. http://coffeetalkswithmessiah.com/ *Jill is also a prophetic musician and singer. Her music is found at*
https://www.youtube.com/channel/UCbxPVDU0bNAomv684flEhHA

Following Shabbat, there are seven Appointed Feasts of the Lord listed in the annual calendar in Leviticus 23.

1. Passover (Lev 23:5)
2. The Feast of Unleavened Bread (Lev 23:6-8)
3. The First Fruits of the Grain Harvest (Lev 23:9-14)
4. The Feast of Weeks (Lev 23:15-22)
5. The Feast of Trumpets (Lev 23:23-25)
6. The Day of Atonement (Lev 23:26-32)
7. The Feast of Tabernacles (Lev 23:33-36, 39-43)

The first four occur in the spring (in the Northern Hemisphere) and the last three in the autumn (fall).

The Three Pilgrimage Festivals

In Exodus, God set apart three pilgrimage festivals which the Israelites were to travel to Jerusalem to celebrate (Ex 23:14-17). The first festival, Passover, was to remember the day when He called the nation into being. *Remember this day in which you went out from Egypt...for by a powerful hand the LORD brought you out from this place* (Ex 13:3). The fathers were to tell their sons and this would be a sign and a reminder of the day of their deliverance (Ex 13:8-9). Passover also includes the seven days of eating unleavened bread and also the first fruits offering which was waved before the Lord on the day after the Sabbath. This began the counting of the Omer (a measure of dry grain), preparing for Pentecost 50 days later. The first fruits were not only the crops but also from the animals and first-born sons, who were to be consecrated and redeemed to remember the first-born of Egypt who died (Ex 13:2,12-15).

The second pilgrimage festival is Shavuot, the Feast of Weeks (Pentecost), which occurs at the time of the grain harvest (barley and wheat). It was a celebration and offering to the Lord of the first ripe barley. Around this time of year, God spoke to Moses and wrote the constitution for the new nation on Mt Sinai.

The third festival which the families had to come to Jerusalem to celebrate is the Feast of Tabernacles. This began with the Feast of Trumpets and these days remind us that God is king and judge of all the earth. On Yom Kippur, two goats were brought to the temple; one was sacrificed while the other was sent into the wilderness carrying the sin away, never to return (Lev chapter 16). Five days later the mood changes to celebration as the final fruit harvest is gathered in. The Feast of Tabernacles or Booths remembers the temporary shelters used during the desert wandering and the Jews eat and even sleep in these for eight days with much rejoicing. We will look at these festivals in more detail as they occur but for now the most important thing is to grasp their prophetic importance.

The Dress Rehearsal

As mentioned above, the word 'mo'ed' also means dress rehearsal. These festivals are a summary of the God's redemption history of Israel and all humanity and each is a sign of an historic event in that story. They are a prophetic map of key events. Note that each of the feasts was fulfilled on the exact day in the biblical calendar.

- At Passover, the lamb was slain and its blood on the lintel caused the angel of death to pass over their houses. At Passover, Jesus, the Lamb of God, was crucified to become the Passover lamb for our sin (Matt 26:2, 1 Cor 5:7)
- As the leaven is removed from the bread at Passover, so Jesus, the sinless one, removed the sin from our lives (Heb 10:12,19-22)
- As the first fruits were brought to the temple on the day after the Sabbath, so Jesus rose from the dead and became the first fruit of the resurrection (1 Cor 15:20-25)
- As the grain was being waved in the Temple at Pentecost, God poured out his Holy Spirit on the disciples gathered in the upper room and their fiery preaching brought in the first fruits of the harvest of the church. Three thousand were saved that day, bringing an offering of life, where 3,000 died at Mt Sinai for their idolatry (Acts 2:1-41).

There is then a long gap over summer, where there are no major events on the biblical calendar until the final harvest is gathered. The autumn/fall feasts are all prophetic of end-time events that are yet to occur but we are right at the doorstep of God once again dramatically breaking into human history.

- The Feast of Trumpets foreshadows the trumpet of God that sounds to call the elect to Himself at the rapture (1 Thess 4:13-18, 1 Cor 15:51-54).
- The Day of Atonement is the day of Israel's repentance when they will recognise Him whom they have pierced (Zech 12:10), most likely associated with the nations coming against them and the time of Jacob's trouble (Jer 30:4-7).

- This repentance will trigger the Messiah to come and dwell amongst His people and rule as King of kings for 1,000 years, represented by the Feast of Tabernacles which is the feast of the nations (Rev 19:11-18, 20:2, Zech 14:3-5).
- The eighth day, Shmini Atzeret, is a holy convocation that foreshadows the end of the 1,000 years and the beginning of the eternal era.

This should help us to see why it is important to enter into God's prophetic timing and celebrate the Feasts of the Lord with the children of Israel. As they change each year, you can check the feast dates in the introduction or look them up on the web at https://www.hebcal.com. It also helps us in our prophetic intercession as we join with our Jewish Messiah and Lord in how He may be praying for His people.

FEAST	OT EVENT	NT EVENT	APPLICATION
PASSOVER Lev 23:5	Redemption from Egypt. Ex 12:1-14)	Redemption – Jesus' death as the Passover Lamb. 1 Cor 5:7	Saved from the kingdom of Satan. Col 1:12-14
UNLEAVENED BREAD Lev 23:6-8	Memorial to leaving the old ways. Overcoming the 'destroyer'. Ex 12:15-20	Jesus destroys death. Sanctification. Leaven = sin and dead religion. Rev 1:17-18, Rom 6:8-11, 1 Cor 5:6-8, Matt 16:6-12	Die to sin. Rom 6:3
FIRST FRUITS Lev 23:9-14	Consecration of the first-born. Redemption of the first-born son. Ex 13:2,12-15	New Birth – Jesus' resurrection. 1 Cor 15:20	Raised with Christ. Rom 6:5
PENTECOST Lev 23:15-22	Giving of the Law on stone – the 3,000 slain. Ex chapter 20ff, 32:28	Outpouring of the Spirit. Birth of the church – 3,000 saved Acts 2:1, 37-41	Holy Spirit given to us. God teaches us His ways. Jn 16:13

FEAST	OT EVENT	NT EVENT	APPLICA-TION
TRUMPETS Lev 23:23-25	The trumpet sounds Ex 19:18-19, Ps 47 The Lord ascends to reign	The Rapture. The Lord descends for His church. 1 Thess 4:16-17, 1 Cor 15:50-53	God calls us to reign with Him. Eph 2:4-6
ATONEMENT Lev 23:26-32	Day of Atonement. Lev 16 Repentance. Isaiah chapter 59, Zech 12:10 Day of Judgement. Joel chapter 2-3	Israel repents. Rom 11:11-12, 25-27 Day of Judgement. 1 Thess 5:1-11, Rev 19:11-21	Die to self – living sacrifice. Rom 12:1-2
TABERNACLES Lev 23:33-36, 39-44	Harvest festival. Deut 16:13-16 God's Kingdom on earth. Zech chapter 14, Ezek 43-48	The Lord dwells among His people. Jn 1:14, Lk 21:25-33, Rev 20:1-6	Become His bride. Rev 19:7

A Prophetic Picture of the End Times – Reuven and Mary-Lou Doron 2008

The Cycles of the End

...The end of the age will see three cycles: *alarm, conviction, and harvest*. The Fall Feasts warn us of these intensifying contractions, as creation travails in the birth pains of Messiah. These three cycles will continue to visit the earth in recurring and intensifying cycles. Whether it will be wars, economic meltdowns, natural disasters, or social upheaval, the trumpets will continue to call for our attention.

And as contrition and conviction mount in search of real rescue and atonement, a wonderful harvest shall be gathered, again and again, among those who hear the sound of God calling, 'Adam, where are you?'

The testimony of the Fall Feasts is one of warning, endurance, repentance, valor and victory, not of denial or escape. The entire body of Scripture and the Messiah's nature consistently point toward the path of endurance, sacrifice, and victory through suffering.

In a vision 26 years ago, we witnessed and experienced the promised 'catching up of the saints to be with the Lord' as, we believe, it will occur (though we have no idea when, and certainly much endurance and suffering will take place in the body of Messiah before then). This fantastic event, as we understand and expect it to be, will take place dramatically and spectacularly at the very end of this present age as one dispensation gives way to the next at the coming of the Lord.

God's people would be wise to observe or learn from the Fall Feasts of the Lord in the Spirit, learn their prophetic implications, act in accordance with the lessons of the feasts, and prepare for the relentless cycles of the end. The Trumpets' *alarms*, leading to Atonement's *conviction* of sin, will produce Tabernacles' *harvests* again and again, as we draw near to the end.

For the Lord Himself will descend from heaven with a shout, with the voice of the archangel, and with the trumpet of God; and the dead in Christ shall rise first. Then we who are alive and remain shall be caught up together with them in the clouds to meet the Lord in the air, and thus we shall always be with the Lord. Therefore comfort one another with these words. Now as to the times and the epochs, brethren, you have no need of anything to be written to you. For you yourselves know full well that the day of the Lord will come just like a thief in the night. While they are saying, 'Peace and safety!' then destruction will come upon them suddenly like birth pangs upon a woman with child; and they shall not escape. But you, brethren, are not in darkness, that the day should overtake you like a thief; for you are all sons of light and sons of day. We are not of night nor of darkness; so then let us not sleep as others do, but let us be alert and sober. 1 Thess 4:16-5:6

Reuven and Mary Lou Doron, originally from the US, are the directors of *'One New Man Call'*. https://www.facebook.com/onenewmancall Reuven is currently the Director of Ministerial Relations for the Sar-El Tour Group in Israel.

Feast Dates 2020-2030

In re-adjusting to a biblical timeframe, the first thing to remember is that days begin at sundown and end the following sundown, so for all the dates given below, the holidays actually begin the night before the date shown. https://www.infoplease.com/calendar-holidays/major-holidays/jewish-holidays

The holidays move in the Western (Gregorian) calendar year since the Jewish calendar is a luni-solar calendar, instead of just a solar calendar. The dates are further complicated by how intercalendary months are calculated and inserted. Dates given for multi-day holidays are for the beginning of the holiday.

The Major Festival Dates are:

	Purim/ Lots	Pesach/ Passover	Shavuot/ Weeks	Rosh HaShanah/ Trumpets	Yom Kippur/ Atonement	Sukkot/ Tabernacles	Hanukka/ Dedication /Lights
2020	Mar 10	April 9	May 29	Sept 19	Sept 28	Oct 3	Dec 11
2021	Feb 26	Mar 28	May 17	Sept 7	Sept 16	Sept 21	Nov 29
2022	Mar 17	April 16	June 5	Sept 26	Oct 5	Oct 10	Dec 19
2023	Mar 7	April 6	May 26	Sept 16	Sept 25	Sept 30	Dec 8
2024	Mar 24	April 23	June 12	Oct 3	Oct 12	Oct 17	Dec 26
2025	Mar 14	April 13	June 2	Sept 23	Oct 2	Oct 7	Dec 15
2026	Mar 3	April 2	May 22	Sept 12	Sept 21	Sept 26	Dec 5
2027	Mar 23	April 22	June 11	Oct 2	Oct 11	Oct 16	Dec 25
2028	Mar 12	April 11	May 31	Sept 21	Sept 30	Oct 5	Dec 13
2029	Mar 1	Mar 31	May 20	Sept 10	Sept 19	Sept 24	Dec 2
2030	Mar 19	April 18	June 7	Sept 28	Oct 7	Oct 12	Dec 21

Length of Jewish holidays:

The length of the different holidays varies somewhat according to the different Jewish branches and whether one lives in Israel or overseas.

Orthodox and Conservative Judaism:

In Israel: Purim: 1 day. Passover: 7 days; first and last are holy. Shavuot: 1 day. Rosh Hashanah: 2 days. Yom Kippur: 1 day. Sukkot: 7 days; first is holy. Shemini Atzeret (8th day of Sukkot): 1 day. Hanukkah: 8 days.

Reform:
Purim: 1 day. Passover: 7 days; first and last are holy. Shavuot: 1 day. Rosh Hashanah: 1 day. Yom Kippur: 1 day. Sukkot: 7 days; first is holy. Shemini Atzeret: 1 day. Hanukkah: 8 days.

Hebrew Months

The names of the Hebrew months are derived from Babylon. The Bible usually used numbers for months (first month, second month...) rather than names. Four names are mentioned in Scripture (in brackets).

1. March/April	Nisan (Abib – Spring)
2. April/May	Iyar (Ziv - light)
3. May/June	Sivan
4. June/July	Tammuz
5. July/August	Av
6. Aug/Sept	Elul
7. Sept/Oct	Tishrei (Ethanim - strong)
8. Oct/Nov	Cheshvan (Marcheshvan or Bul - eighth)
9. Nov/Dec	Kislev
10. Dec/Jan	Tevet
11. Jan/Feb	Shevat
12. Feb/March	Adar
13.	Adar II (leap year)

Sound of the Shofar

Photo courtesy David Nesher

May the sound of the shofar shatter our complacency
And make us conscious of the corruption in our lives.

May the sound of the shofar penetrate our souls
And cause us to turn back to our Father in Heaven.

May the sound of the shofar break the bonds of the evil impulse within us
And enable us to serve the Lord with a whole heart.

May the sound of the shofar renew our loyalty to the one true King
And strengthen our determination to defy the false gods.

May the sound of the shofar awaken us to the enormity of our sins
And the vastness of God's mercy for those who truly repent.

May the sound of the shofar summon us to service
And stir us to respond, as did Abraham, 'Here am I.'

May the sound of the shofar recall the moment
When we stood at Mount Sinai and uttered the promise:
'All that the Lord has spoken, we will keep and obey.'

May the sound of the shofar recall the promise of the ingathering of the exiles
And stir within us renewed devotion to the Land of Israel.

May the sound of the shofar recall the vision of the prophets,
Of the day when Egypt, Syria and Israel will live in peace.

May the sound of the shofar awaken us to the flight of time
And summon us to spend our days with purpose.

May the sound of the shofar become our jubilant shout of joy
On the day of the promised, long-awaited redemption.

May the sound of the shofar remind us that it is time
To 'proclaim liberty throughout the land to all the inhabitants thereof.'

May the sound of the shofar enter our hearts;
For blessed is the people that hearkens to its call.

From a devotional found in a traditional High Holy Day prayer supplement in an Orthodox synagogue. Quoted in Nesher, H., Messiah Revealed in the Fall Feasts, *Nesher Pub, 2004, Edmonton, Canada, P 16,17. Hannah has a teaching ministry.* https://www.voiceforisrael.net

The Monthly Prayer Focus

All Israel Shall be Saved

January

Israel's Glorious Destiny

For Zion's sake I will not keep silent, for Jerusalem's sake I will not rest, until her righteousness shines out brightly, and her salvation as a blazing torch. Nations will see your righteousness, and all kings your glory. Isaiah 62:1-2a (Tree of Life Version)

The kings of the earth take their stand and the rulers take counsel together against the Lord and against His Anointed...But...I have installed My King upon Zion, My holy mountain. Ps 2:2,6

January

In January, we look at Israel's calling, purpose and destiny and our part in this. We ask why we should pray for Israel specifically and see some of the spiritual forces that seek to impede this destiny. We then pray some of the prophetic promises God has for His people, His land and Jerusalem.

Every person and every nation is created for a unique purpose. We are called to walk in that purpose and fulfil our destiny and I believe we will be judged according to how closely we have done that. But how many of us know our individual calling? Even less likely, how many of us understand God's purpose for our nation? We cannot fulfil something until we have a concept of what we are trying to create. Our destiny does not start with ourselves but begins when we turn to the Lord and dedicate our lives to Him. He can then begin to lead and teach us the master plan God has ordained for our lives.

Your eyes have seen my unformed substance; and in Your book were all written the days that were ordained for me, when as yet there was not one of them. Ps 139:16

For we are His workmanship, created in Christ Jesus for good works, which God prepared beforehand so that we would walk in them. Eph 2:10

In our Western thinking, we see everything on an individual basis and interpret Scripture accordingly. However, Middle Eastern thinking in ancient times, and even today, is corporate. A person was part of a tribe, a people group, a nation and this gives the individual their identity. Nations also have a unique purpose especially Israel. God called Abraham and He obeyed. God promised to make him a multitude of nations (Gen 17:5). He called Moses to bring the Hebrew people out of Egypt and He made them a nation at Mt Sinai, personally delivering their national constitution and legal system. Their purpose was to redeem the nations that fell at Babel (Greek – Babylon) in Gen 11:1-9 by being a blessing and bringing light to the Gentile nations (Gen 12:1-3, Is 49:6). The Jewish people have birthed Jesus and brought the gospel of salvation to the nations. This was the outcome of His first visit, but there are also Scriptures that say He will come as a glorious King to rule the nations as the Prince of Peace. As this is Jesus' destiny, we are invited to participate in the preparation for this earth-shattering event. Our destiny and Israel's are inseparable from Jesus' destiny if we have united our hearts with His.

Why Pray for the Jewish People?

While we need to pray for all people groups, the Word attests that God chose the Jews to fulfil a specific purpose. If the coming of the Messiah as Saviour were the end of the story for the nation of Israel (or the church), we could all be transported to Heaven as soon as we received Jesus as our Saviour. This does not happen, because salvation is not just individual, but the coming of the Kingdom of God involves the destiny of nations (Matt 25:32, Ezek 35:7-11, Joel 3:12 etc). God's measuring stick for the judgement of nations is their attitude towards Israel!

The ultimate aim of God's love for all nations is that 'they shall know that I am the Lord' (Joel 3:16-17). Jews understand being a 'light to the nations' (Is 42:6) in the concept of 'Tikkun Olam' – repairing the world. The world has been blessed by their incredible record of winning Nobel prizes at a rate far exceeding their size. Jews constitute barely 2% of the world's population yet have won 20% of all Nobel prizes. They are always on the cutting edge of using their God-given talents to make the world a better place and sharing that with others. While other religions and philosophies are advocating wiping out those who do not agree with their religious views, or looking inward and teaching how to escape this world by blocking it out, or how to accumulate wealth for selfish means, the Jews are looking outward, pre-occupied with preparing the way for a better world for everyone.

Only when the Jewish nation is spiritually united to its God will it reach its full potential. We can be encouraged by seeing that the Messianic congregations are growing and multiplying, and that there are more Jews coming to the Lord now than ever in history since Biblical times. The Lord has been faithful to His covenant and kept a remnant to this day. He is once again regathering His people so they are an identifiable nation. The work is far from finished as only half the world's Jewish population have come home and most of those regathered are yet to believe. However, the congregations in Israel are flourishing, despite (or maybe because of) the opposition. The Lord will return to Israel after a period of desolation when Jerusalem again welcomes her King (Matt 23:37-39). The stage is once again being set for an occasion as momentous in history, as the resurrection of Jesus, but it cannot be fulfilled until the Jewish people are ready.

Garden Tomb, Jerusalem

The Calling of the Gentile Nations

This is where the Gentiles come in. Jesus commissioned His followers to go and take the gospel of God's kingdom to the ends of the earth before the end would come (Matt 24:14). This part the church has understood, even if it has not always been very diligent in obeying. It was to go to the Jew first (Rom 1:16), which the first disciples did, although it has not been carried through to our day. What has not been clearly understood is the crucial role the Gentiles must play in making the Jews jealous, so they will want to return to God. The good news for a Jew is when someone reminds them that *"Your God reigns"*.

> *How lovely on the mountains are the feet of him who brings good news*
> *Who announces peace and brings good news of happiness*
> *Who announces salvation and says to Zion, "Your God reigns".*
>
> Is 52:7

For most of Christian history, we have accepted Israel's God, claimed Him for ourselves to the exclusion of the Jews, or forced them to convert to Christianity – meaning that they must give up all their Jewish traditions, often to trade them for more pagan-based practices. We have forgotten that Jesus was Jewish and actually kept all those Biblical 'traditions'. Paul warned us of this arrogance and reminded the Gentiles that they were only 'grafted in' and that although the Jews had been cut off for their unbelief, God was perfectly capable of re-grafting the original branches back in (Rom 11:23-24). It is only a matter of time until God's prophetic word will be fulfilled (Rom 11:25-26). Our prayers, coupled with the practical demonstration of our love will not only make a difference to the Jewish people but also hasten the coming of the Messiah.

With the ongoing troubles in the Middle East, we see more and more how the central core of the conflict centres on Jerusalem, just as the Biblical prophets said it would in the end times (Zech 12:1-7, 14:1-4, Is 66:7-23, Dan 11:36-12:4, Joel 3:12-17, Micah 4:1-13). I believe that the promised restoration is a process, not an event. We are fortunate to be living in the days that these prophets longed to see; when the fulfilment has begun. If we are looking for an event, we may miss the mighty things that God is already bringing to pass. One of the aims of the *Jewish and Israel Prayer Focus* is to give us a glimpse into that restoration and encourage us to search the Scriptures and see how they are being fulfilled. As the Lord opens our eyes to see this relationship, He is also inviting us to be a part of this restoration process. There are many opportunities provided in this book for us to stay in touch with Jewish and Gentile believers in Israel, and become involved through relationship, prayer and practical help. Our prayers need feet and our hearts need to be felt. The world wide web is a wonderful tool. Let us be a blessing to God's people, and we will reap the eternal rewards (Gen 12:3, Matt 25:31-45).

January

Why Pray for Israel?

1. *The King is coming to Jerusalem.* On His return, Jesus will plant His feet on the Mount of Olives, from where He left this earth (Zech 14:4,9, Acts 1:11-12). We are invited to participate in the preparation of the way for His arrival.

2. *He will not come until the Jewish people welcome Him* from where they denied Him (Matt 23:37-39). Jesus wept over Jerusalem after He had declared the woes over the Pharisees who had so distorted the meaning of His law with their hypocritical attitudes. He then decreed the desolation of Jerusalem *until* they once again welcomed Him. The Messianic greeting from Ps 118:26 'blessed is He who comes in the name of the Lord', is still used today and is the Hebrew way of saying 'welcome'. Just as the Father commanded His people to come up to Jerusalem during the prophetic feasts of Passover and Weeks so they would witness His death, resurrection and the outpouring of the Spirit on the first believers, so today He is gathering His children from across the globe and returning them to Israel to witness His soon coming to fulfil the third pilgrim Feast of Tabernacles. He does not want a secular nation but promises to cleanse them, forgive their sin, give them new hearts and write His law on their hearts (Ezek 36:26-27, Jer 32:31-34).

3. *We are commanded to pray for the peace of Jerusalem.* There are only two cities we are commanded in Scripture to pray for – Jerusalem in Ps 122:6 and the one in which we reside (Jer 29:7).

4. *If we love the Lord and pray for Him to align our hearts with His, then we will love the people and the things that are on His heart.* He loves His people with an everlasting love (Jer 31:3).

5. *God has ordained Israel for a unique purpose given to no other country.* He has made eternal covenants with Israel and they must therefore be fulfilled (Gen 17:1-7, Jer 31:31-36). If He were to break His Word with His people Israel because of their disobedience, then we have no assurance of salvation,

as we also stand on His Covenant Word sealed with His blood. Surely we have not been any more obedient than Israel? But for His grace...

6. *We are grafted in to the olive tree of Israel*, bonded with our elder brother in the Lord. Romans chapters 9-11 spell this out. The destiny of the church and the destiny of Israel are now intertwined. We need to build together the One New Man in Christ (Eph 2:11-22).

7. *The church is God's conduit to bring the Jews back to the land and to their Lord.* We are to pray for their salvation, demonstrate God's love, preach the gospel, bring His people back to the land on our shoulders, and make them jealous with our love for the God of the Israel and point them to their own Messiah (Is 49:22, 52:7, Rom 1:16, 10:19, 11:11).

8. *We owe the Jewish people a debt* as they have given us the Scriptures, our Lord and the knowledge of salvation (Rom 15:27). As we have received, we are now part of God's answer to show our gratitude and give back to them.

9. *Jesus was and is Jewish.* He has never changed his race and never will. True Christianity is rooted in true Judaism. Christianity has gone astray since it has severed itself from its roots and become proud, arrogant and anti-Semitic. We have made a false Jesus not always aligned with the Scriptures. We need to come back to the roots (Rom 9:1-5).

10. *He will return as a Jewish bridegroom for His bride*, so we had better understand His culture and ways (Rev 19:7). In Revelation chapter 21, it is a new, holy Jerusalem that comes from heaven, not one based in Babylon and its worldly ways.

How Should we then Pray?

- Prepare our own hearts –
    i) Repent – purify our hearts and make them ready
    ii) Understand His end-time purposes – study the Scriptures
    iii) Participate in His end-time plan – action

January

- Pray the yet-to-be fulfilled Scriptures into being
- Pray for and support the work of God in Israel among the Messianic Jewish and Christian Arab congregations and ministries.

Israel, like other western nations, has many of the same challenges – abortion, sodomy, drugs, and the Left wing that want to give land away for a false peace that has not worked to date and is not likely to. Greek apostle and intercessor George Markakis from the *Shalom Athens* prayer ministry wrote about the Greek spirit that is behind Western democracies.

The Prince of Greece – George Markakis 2015

For I have bent Judah, My (bow), fitted the bow with Ephraim, and raised up your sons, O Zion, against your sons, O Greece, and made you like the sword of a mighty man. Zech 9:13

Zechariah's contrast between Judah and Greece identifies a struggle between two arch enemies. Daniel 8:20-21 gives further insight: *The ram which you saw, having the two horns (are) the kings of Media and Persia. And the male goat (is) the kingdom of Greece...* Daniel's prophecy was historically fulfilled by Alexander the Great. The purpose of his conquest was to spread the Hellenic language, culture, religion, and philosophy among the barbarian tribes. But Daniel's words are not only about historical events. He identified the *spirit* that empowered Alexander, who was a disciple of Aristotle and whose mentor was Plato from Athens: human wisdom (philosophy).

Paul identified the nature of the 'Greek spirit' in 1 Cor 1:17-25; *Greeks seek after wisdom.* Jesus confronted the 'Greek spirit' in Matt 11:18-19 ...*wisdom is justified by her children.* That is the wisdom that James called 'earthly, sensual, demonic' (James 3:15). Furthermore, Greece played a pivotal role in the spiritual history of the ancient Mediterranean world, and also of the Western world. Through the Enlightenment, Greek thinking shaped contemporary education and philosophy. Western culture, thought, prevailing philosophy and the political systems are based on the spiritual environment of ancient Athens. One book, Plato's *Republic*, is the spiritual source behind,

All Israel Shall be Saved

and foundation of, all western democratic systems and social order.

While the Greek language has been the chosen vehicle for the New Testament, and Greek culture was predominant during the Roman Empire in which the church was developed, the Greek spirit was also at work to undermine the establishment of God's Kingdom through deviations from the original course, caused by human wisdom.

Daniel 10:20 reveals Satan's strategy: the spirit of Persia came first, bringing violence, intimidation and bloodshed. When Satan could no longer restrain the expansion of the Gospel, he deployed the spirit of Greece. After Constantine, the living Body that was the 'Ecclesia' of Christ governed by anointed leaders and led by the Holy Spirit, became a dead institutional Church, ruled by the state and governed by theologically educated priests teaching about God, thus replacing the living relationship with Jesus.

The Greek spirit works to replace God's wisdom and revelation through theological indoctrination based on rational thinking and human intelligence. It then removes the understanding of God's people Israel through earthly wisdom aiming to *destroy mighty men and the holy people*, as Daniel prophesied in Dan 8:24. That was Satan's original intent - to destroy Israel! This is the spiritual confrontation between Greece and Zion!

George E Markakis is the director of the 'Shalom Center' House of Prayer in Athens, Greece https://www.facebook.com/ShalomCenterAthens

---

In addition to the spiritual challenges of Western countries, Israel has physical challenges that no other nation has: surrounded by those who want to see her annihilated fuelled by the Islamic spirit; the enemies in the UN

January

that target Israel; the Boycott, Divestment and Sanctions (BDS) movement that is trying (unsuccessfully) to cripple Israel economically; and a strong religious spirit that is trying to keep the gospel at bay.

Messianic believer and intercessor, Arni Klein, who has led a 24/7 House of Prayer in Israel wrote:

Spiritual Forces over Israel – Arni Klein 2015

Scripture tells us that there is a hierarchy of unseen spiritual forces whose activities affect our lives on a daily basis. Satan, knowing that the opening of Israel's eyes will light the fuse of his demise, will hold nothing back to stop that happening. We present an overall strategy that delineates three particular principalities to be encountered on the way to Yeshua's return.

Throughout history, religion has been used to blind, manipulate, and control people. We understand this to be the work of a spiritual force we call the 'religious spirit'. Under its dominion are untold millions of souls. Promoting a subtly twisted idea of God, it enslaves people through pride and fear to further the goals of the kingdom of darkness. We believe that the stronghold of this spirit is in Jerusalem – the site of the final battle.

The power next in line promotes the exaltation of man. We know this force as humanism or the 'Greek spirit'. Those in its grip desire to be seen as the best, the richest, the smartest etc. This spirit leads people to lift themselves up by putting others down. We believe the stronghold in Israel of this force is in the Tel Aviv area.

The third, the one we feel is the weakest of the three, and therefore the first to be confronted, is a spirit of false religion. People deceived by this power know the visible

Grave of Rabbi Yohanan Ben Zakai

world is not all there is and are open to spiritual things. Many are lovers of truth. When the light comes they will turn to the Lord. We perceive the stronghold of this power in Israel is in Galilee, where Yeshua spent most of His life. This region includes 1) Haifa, where Elijah battled the false prophets of Baal and is today the world headquarters of the Bahai, 2) Safed, the world center for Kabala - an occultic form of Jewish mysticism, and 3) Tiberias, to where tens of thousands flock to worship at the tombs of three of the most influential rabbis who established rabbinical Judaism, a system where the writings and opinions of men supersede the Torah – essentially creating a false religion.

This is the region mentioned in Isaiah 9:1-2 where the people walking in darkness see a great light. Could it be that, as it was with Yeshua's first appearance, so the light of His glory will again emanate from the north? We believe so. In keeping with this understanding of God's strategic plan, we are inviting groups from the nations to come and join worshippers from across Galilee to prepare the way of the Lord in Israel.

Arni and Yonit Klein have previously pioneered places of worship in the regions of Tel Aviv and Jerusalem. http://emmausway.org *If you would like to participate in a gathering in the Galilee you go to:* https://galilee-worship.com. *They have also produced a 10 session course designed for small groups.* https://www.israelrevealed.org

Israel's Prophetic Destiny

In praying the destiny of nations and therefore the Kingdom of God to earth, we should be pray as Abraham did and remind God of His promises. We do not have to look very far in the Bible to find promises for the nation of Israel. Israel's prophetic future and destiny are most clearly set out in Ezekiel chapters 36-37 and Jeremiah chapters 31-33. In brief, they promise:

January

- a physical regathering from exile and return to the land for the sake of God's name – His covenants must be fulfilled
- a restoration of the land and the cities
- a cleansing of the hearts and forgiveness of their sins
- a new covenant: new heart and a new spirit with the law written on their hearts. *They will know that I am the Lord*
- a new marriage relationship - *They will be my people and I will be their God*

January Prayer Points – God's Promises to Israel

Here are a few prophetic Scriptures to pray. I suggest praying the whole section, not just the verse.

THE PEOPLE OF ISRAEL

1. I will be your God and you will be My people. Ezek 36:28, 37:23,27.
2. God's own possession. Ps 135:4
3. Israel, My son. Jer 31:20, Hos 11:1
4. You shall be to Me a kingdom of priests. Ex 19:5,6
5. A holy nation, set apart. Deut 26:16-19, Num 23:9
6. You are My witnesses. Isaiah 43:10-12, 44:8
7. You will be a light to (for) the nations. Is 42:6, 49:6
8. The apple of My eye. Deut 32:10, Zech 2:8,
9. My chosen. Is 41:8, 44:1
10. A blessing in all the earth. Is 19:24-25, Gen 12:2-3
11. I will give you a new heart. Ezek 36:26
12. I will put My Spirit within you. Ezek 36:27, 37:1-14
13. Your hearts will be cleansed. Ezek 36:33
14. Your sins will be forgiven. Jer 31:34, Zech 13:1

THE LAND OF ISRAEL

15. The desert shall blossom. Is chapter 35
16. The people will return. Ezek 36:24

All Israel Shall be Saved

17. The cities will be rebuilt. Ezek 36:33
18. The productivity of the land will be restored. Ezek 36:30, 34,35
19. The priesthood will be cleansed. Mal 3:3
20. There will be singing and dancing in the streets and your young men will dream dreams and old men will see visions. Jer 31:4,13, Joel 2:28-32

THE CITY OF JERUSALEM

21. City of Righteousness. Is 1:26
22. A praise in all the earth. Is 62:7
23. My dwelling place and the place of My throne. Ezek 43:7
24. City of the Great King. Ps 48:2
25. My Holy Mountain. Is 56:7, 65:25, 66:20, Joel 3:17
26. City of Truth. Zech 8:3
27. Holy City. Is 52:1
28. City of God. Ps 46:4
29. A cup of reeling and a heavy stone. Zech 12:1-5
30. The seat of the Lord's rulership over the nations. Zech 14:4-9
31. The New Jerusalem. Rev chapter 21

February
Seeds of Faith in the Land

My heart's desire and my prayer to God for them is their salvation. For I testify about them that they have a zeal for God, but not in accordance with knowledge. For not knowing about God's righteousness and seeking to establish their own, they did not subject themselves to the righteousness of God. For Christ is the goal of the law for righteousness to everyone who believes. Romans 10:1-4

I tell you that in the same way there will be more rejoicing in heaven over one sinner who repents than over ninety-nine righteous persons who do not need to repent. Luke 15:7 (NIV)

February

Congregations in the Land

In February, we try to make a spiritual map of the Land, looking at where the congregations are and where gaps exist that need to be prayed for. Specific prayer points from the congregations are sent out every two months in the Jewish and Israel Prayer Letter, to which you are welcome to sign up. Contact watchmen777@optusnet.com.au.

The good news is that this list is not complete and can never be complete because God is at work, multiplying and expanding the congregations, new ones being planted first as home groups which then grow, and this does not include the traditional Christian churches that have been in the Land for many years, or no doubt many secret believers whom God alone knows. Many ministries, such as Voice of Judah in Ashdod, Tents of Mercy in Haifa, and Revive Israel in Tel Aviv are constantly reaching out and planting new branches. There are more Jewish believers in Israel now than at any time since the biblical era and it is increasing! The 'times of the Gentiles' are slowly being transformed once again into the 'times of the Jews', preparing to welcome the Messiah back as King.

Geographical Areas of Israel

1. North & Jezreel Valley
2. Centre
3. Coastal Plains
4. Judea, Samaria, Gaza
5. Jerusalem
6. South.

Jesus said to his disciples:

And you will be hated by all on account of My name, but it is the one who has endured to the end who will be saved. But whenever they persecute you

All Israel Shall be Saved

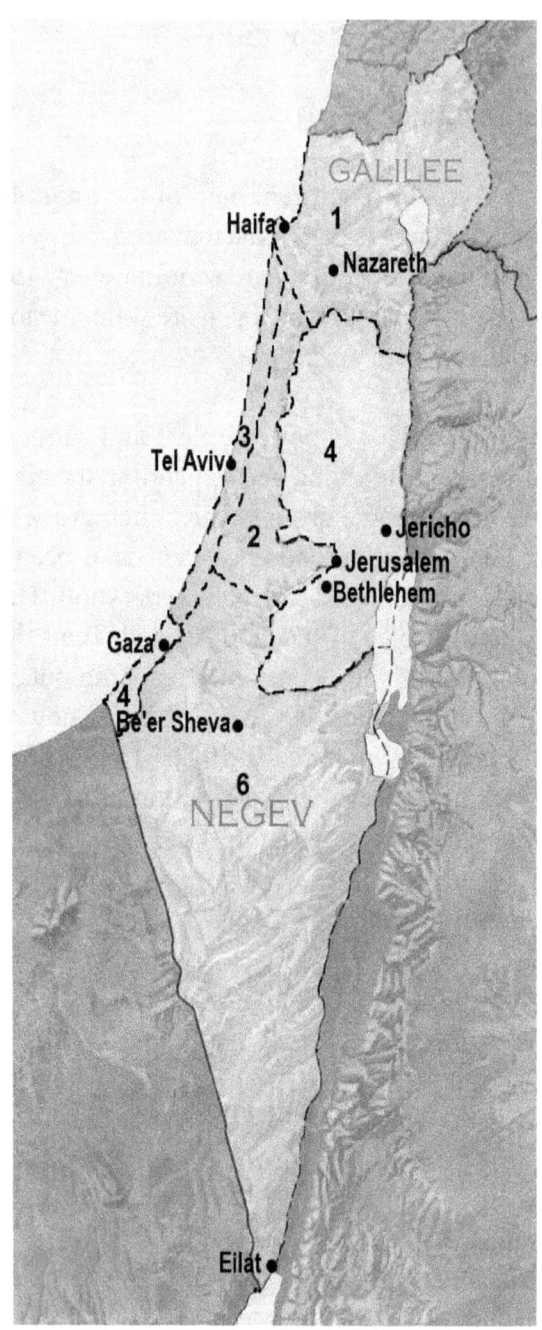

Original base map courtesy of U.S. Central Intelligence Agency via www.lib.utexas.edu

February

in this city, flee to the next; for truly I say to you, you shall not finish going through the cities of Israel, until the Son of Man comes. Matt 10:22-23

The disciples were sent out to the cities of Israel and warned it would not be an easy task. They would not be welcomed in every place. However, they were commanded in Matt 10:7-8 to preach the gospel that the Kingdom of Heaven was at hand, to heal the sick, raise the dead, cleanse the lepers, cast out demons and give freely as they had received.

Let us pray:

- for the establishment of the living witness of a congregation that will preach the true gospel boldly with the accompaniment of signs and wonders in every city of Israel. You may like to look up in a concordance some of the Scriptures about these cities as part of your prayers.
- that there will be strong Biblical teaching and no false doctrines
- for unity between the believers
- for the One New Man of Arab and Jew to arise and witness together
- for spiritual growth to maturity and numerical growth in the congregations
- for the youth to be strong in their faith and witness especially as they serve in the army
- for God to draw people to the congregations and find the on-line resources
- for opportunities to share the gospel as they offer humanitarian aid
- the Body of Messiah in the Land. It is at a stage of the transference of leadership in many congregations from the pioneers, who were often born overseas and immigrated, to the next generation who were born in the Land and speak Hebrew as a first language. Pray for these young leaders to have great wisdom, anointing, compassion and insight as they rise up and take the reins

The years noted are the years when this congregation was featured in the *Jewish (and Israel) Prayer Focus booklet*. A great resource for congregations can be found at https://app.kehila.org/congregations. They list 72 congregations in Israel.

All Israel Shall be Saved

1. Congregations in the North - Galilee/Jezreel Valley

Afula

1. Kehilat Emek Yisrael – Hannah Haustein 2010, 2018
2. Heart of Megiddo (Russian) – Michael and Nataly Milevsky 2019 https://isravalley.org

Akko

Harvest of Asher – Ps Guy Cohen 2006 http://harvestofasher.org

Beit Shean

Spirit of Life Congregation – Ps Eliav Levin 2010, 2016

Nazareth

1. Netzer HaGalil – Branch of Galilee (Russian) – Ps Leon Mazin, Nazareth Ellit 2016   info@shaveitzion.org, http://english.shaveitzion.org
2. Hebrew congregation – Yakov Dolinsky 2009, 2012

Haifa/Mt Carmel/Kiryat Yam

1. Kerem El (God's Vineyard) – Stefan Silver 2008, 2013, 2016 office@ kerem-el.org.il   http://www.kerem-el.org
2. Kehilat HaCarmel (Carmel Assembly - Isufia) – Dani Sayag and Peter Tsukahira 2002, 2011, 2017 https://www.carmelcongregation.org.il
3. Retzon Ha'el (God's will – Ethiopian) – Zechariah Arni 2013
4. Tents of Mercy – Ps Eitan Shishkoff. Humanitarian aid and congregation planting. Now with five congregations Nazareth, Haifa, Tiberias, Akko and their home congregation in Kiriyat Yam (Ps Avishalom Teklehaimanot) on Haifa Bay 2002, 2005 https://www.tentsofmercy.org
5. The Immanuel Church, Haifa – Ps Najeeb and Elizabeth Atteih (Arab) 2019

February

6. House of Light (Shefa Amer) – Ps Anis and Nawal Barhoum (Arab) 2019
   http://www.houseoflight.net

Nahariya

1. Kehilat Or HaGalil – Ps Ephraim Goldstein (Ruth Nessim) 2003, 2004, 2017
2. River of God Lebanese Congregation – Ps Joseph Hadad 2007, 2018

Karmiel

1. Kehilat HaDerek - The Way Congregation – Ps Yossi Ovadia 2008
   http://www.kehilathaderech.org/english
2. Living Israel – Ps Eli Dorfman http://livingkarmiel.com

Kiryat Shemona

A home group started here from Karmiel fellowship.

Shaar HaEmek

Shaar HaEmek Congregation – begun by Ps Israel Harel until 2013. Current status unknown

Tiberias/Poriya

1. Morning Star Fellowship – Ps Claude Ezagouri 2006, 2013
   https://shepherdstaffministries.org/morning-star-fellowship-tiberias
2. Kehilat HaNahar – Ps Aviel & Nirit Gersh 2017
3. The Poriya Congregation – Eric and Terri Morey (Ronnen and Svetlana Venter) 2003, 2007 https://www.kehilatporiya.org
4. Peniel Fellowship – Ps Daniel Yahav 2003, 2009, 2017
   https://www.penielfellowshipisrael.com

2. Congregations in the Centre of the Land

Beit Shemesh

Kehilat Keren Tikva (Ray of Hope) – Sidney and Linda Speakman 2003. Sidney and Linda Speakman started a ministry here that had a congregation. They were forced to leave the country, but I believe others are now leading it.

Kfar Saba

HaMaayan Congregation – Ps Tony Sperandeo 2004, 2016
http://www.kehilat-hamaayan.org.il

Modi'in

Kehilat Modi'in – Ray Pritz 2010

Rehovot

Rehovot Messianic Fellowship – Ps Jacob 2011, 2018

Ramle/Lod

1. Calling of Israel – Ps Ariel Revach 2019
http://mountmoriah.org.uk/dvd-videos/video-messages-from-the-pastors.html
2. Beit Hallel (House of Praise) 2012

3. Congregations in the Coastal Plains

Ashdod

Beit Hallel – Ps Israel Pochtar 2019 https://beit-hallel.org

February

Ashkelon

1. Kehilat Shekhinah Congregation (Spanish) – Ps Daniel Borenstejn 2017
2. Beit Hallel in Ashdod is planting a congregation here also
https://vojisrael.org/plant_ashkelon

Herzliyya

King of Kings Assembly Herzliyya – Ps Daniel 2019 https://www.kkch.org

Netanya

Beit Asaph – Ps Evan Thomas and Lev Guler 2002, 2004, 2009, 2013, 2015, https://beit-asaph.org.il/about

Rishon L'Zion

1. Avney Nezer (Awake Israel) – Ps Shlomy Abramov 2018
http://www.awakeisrael.org.il
2. Tehilat-yah (God's praise) – Michael Yaron 2014, 2018
http://tehilat-yah.org

Tel Aviv/Jaffa/Bat Yam

1. Belay Birlie – Ethiopian Congregations 2006, 2008, 2012
https://firstcenturyfoundations.com/ethiopian-congregations-in-israel
2. Beit Immanuel – Rev Aleksey Raikhstadt (David Lazarus - founder) 2002, 2007, 2016, https://www.messianic-jews.org
3. Beit Yeshua (House of Yeshua) – Ps Neriyah Arabov (Russian) Bat Yam 2016
4. Dugit Congregation – Ps Avi Mizrachi 2003, 2004, 2016
https://www.dugit.org/who-we-are
5. Gospel to the Nations Church – Sibhat Petros (Eritrean) 2018
6. Living Stone Ministries Israel – Daniel Rozen 2010
israel_jfls@yahoo.com
https://www.facebook.com/HOFIsrael http://livingstoneministriesisrael.com

7. New Covenant Church – Gabriel Bezuneh/Robel Wolderchiros (Ethiopian) 2018
8. Sacred Assembly – Ps Baruch and Karen Maayan. The congregation that meets from the Trumpet of Salvation Ministry 2016
9. Tiferet Yeshua Congregation – Ps Ari Sorko Ram and Kobi and Shani Ferguson 2003 https://maozisrael.org

4. Congregations in Judea, Samaria & Gaza

Ariel

1. Messianic Jewish fellowship – Ps David and Leah Ortiz 2009
2. Tikvat Shomron (Hope of Samaria) – Henry and Irena N. Chosen People Ministries Congregation

Bethlehem

1. First Baptist Church (Arab) – Ps Naim Khoury http://fbc-bethlehem.org
2. Bethlehem Bible College is here, but is steeped in Replacement Theology.

Gaza

Gaza Baptist Church (Arab) – Ps Hanna Massad http://cm2g.org/main

Jericho

There is at least one born-again Arab pastor working here.

5. Congregations in Jerusalem

Jerusalem

1. Ahavat Yeshua – Ps Asher Intrater 2008, 2011
   http://ahavatyeshuajerusalem.org
2. Beth El Congregation – Ps Tal Shiferow (Ethiopian) 2010

February

3. Calvary Chapel – Brad Antolovich 2003 https://forzion.com
4. Chazon Yerushalaim (Jerusalem Vision) – Ps Shmuel and Pamela Suran 2010 http://jerusalemvision.com
5. Congregation of the Lamb on Mt Zion (Kehilat ha'she al Har Zion) – Pastors Reuven and Benjamin Berger – (Christ Church Hebrew Congregation) 2012, 2013 https://www.christchurchjerusalem.org
6. El Roi'i – Ps Ofer Amitai 2006 https://www.elroii.org/english.html
7. Jerusalem Assembly – Meno Kalisher http://jerusalemassembly.com
8. King of Kings Community Jerusalem (English) – Ps Chad Holland 2007, 2015 http://www.kkcj.org
9. King of Kings Community (Hebrew congregation) – Ps Oded Shoshani 2014, Hebrew@kkcj.org http://www.kkcj.org/ministries/hebrew-congregation
10. Shemen Sasson (Oil of Joy) – Ps Yonathan Almeida 2013 http://shemensasson.com, office@shemensasson.com
11. The Messianic Assembly – Ps Samuel Smadja 2015 https://maozisraelarchive.flywheelsites.com/magazine_issues/july-2016

6. Congregations in the South

Arad

Kehilat Hasdey Yeshua – Ps Jo and Debbie Finkelstein 2018
http://hasdeyyeshua.com

Be'er Sheva

1. Nachalat Yeshua – Ps Howard Bass 2003, 2017
https://www.streamsinthenegev.com
2. House of Grace – Dimitry and Elvira Brodkin (Russian) 2014, 2016
https://firstcenturyfoundations.com/grace-house
3. Desert Flowers – Dov Bikas (Russian) 2014
https://www.avivministry.com/en

All Israel Shall be Saved

Eilat

1. Kehilat Maayan Eilat – Ps Ariel Ben David 2017, 2019
   https://www.maayaneilat.com
2. The Eilat Congregation – Ps John and Judy Pex 2008
   https://firstcenturyfoundations.com/eilat-messianic-congregation-the-shelter

Kiryat Gath

Ps Eitan Manpal – Kiryat Gat Messianic Congregation. Home group planted by Beit Hallel 2013

Sderot

1. Ir HaChayim (City of the Living) – Ps Michael and Dina Beener 2019
   https://www.cityoflifeisrael.com https://news.kehila.org/city-of-life-in-every-sense-of-the-word
2. Repairer of the Ruins Congregation. Also ministering in Ofakim and Netivot

It is suggested that you familiarise yourself with some of these congregations and make a personal connection through a newsletter so you can pray for them. You will notice that none of the Ethiopian congregations have websites. This is largely because they are generally the poorest in the country, have not been raised in a computer society and have few Western contacts with whom they can communicate due to lack of English skills. There are a couple of organisations assisting them: The Sheba Foundation http://www.sheba.org.il and Mount Moriah Trust https://mountmoriah.org.uk.

You will notice that the inner mountainous part of the country of Judea and Samaria, commonly known as 'West Bank' has very few congregations. The 'settlers', who have the pioneering spirit and the biblical conviction who have moved here, have done so mostly because they believe that God has given them the Land and they are therefore claiming it. This is very important as there are about seven million more Jews who have yet to return to the land, so it is needed to absorb them. Those who live in Judea

February

and Samaria (the heartland of the nation in biblical times) are largely traditional, religious Jews and while welcoming Christian support, they strongly oppose any Jew who 'converts' to Christianity, so it is very hard territory for believers to break into (see August). There are some settlements that are secular. Because of the heated political controversy over this part of the land, the Israeli government gives them little support but President Trump is trying to change this political scenario with his 'Deal of the Century'.

February Prayer Points

Romans chapters 9-11 is a key passage in the New Testament confirming that God has *not* finished with Israel and still has a plan for the nation in contrast to the teaching of Replacement Theology, which asserts that God has finished with the Jews and the church is now the new Israel in God's purposes. This month we will focus on praying through this passage. We will look at chapters 9-10 here and chapter 11 later.

Romans 9: The remnant will be saved by faith, not by the law.

1. v 1-3 Pray for us and the church to have God's heart for His Jewish people as Paul did and be willing to sacrifice to see the harvest of the Jews come in.
2. v 4 Pray for Israel to realise and value her unique inheritance to be called sons of God and be entrusted with God's glory, the covenants, the Torah, the temple service and the promises.
3. v 5 Pray for Israel to recognise that Yeshua is their most precious gift from God according to the prophets – from the line of David, the tribe of Judah, born in Bethlehem, as the Saviour for their sins.
4. v 6-7 Pray for the Jews to be aware that God's promise came through Isaac, not Ishmael. Many Jews are duped by the multi-faith propaganda and believe all religions follow the same god. Pray for God to remove their blinders!
5. v 8 Pray for us and Israel to realise what it means to be 'children of promise'.

All Israel Shall be Saved

6. v 9-13 Only that which is born supernaturally of God (Isaac), not born of the flesh (Ishmael – mankind's human good ideas) will prevail. Pray for Israel and us all to know God's word and align ourselves with what God has said must come to pass. Is 55:11
7. v 14-18 Pray for Israel and us to position ourselves to be recipients of God's mercy and compassion because we know and walk in His ways.
8. v 19-20. Pray for Israel and us to be mouldable in the potter's hands.
9. v 21-22 Pray for Israel and us to fulfil our full potential in God in whatever part of the body He has called us to serve.
10. v 23 Pray for us and Israel to be vessels to demonstrate the 'riches of His glory'.
11. v 24 Pray for us – Jews and Gentiles – who are called by His name, to comprehend what it means to be 'vessels of mercy prepared beforehand for His glory'.
12. v 25-26 Israel was cut off for her disobedience but her restoration is assured. Pray for those still physically and spiritually cut off to return.
13. v 27-28 Pray for the remnant to come in according to God's word, 'thoroughly and quickly'.
14. v 29 Praise God that the Jews will never be wiped out as Sodom and Gomorrah were. Jer 31:35-36.
15. v 30-33 May Israel realise that salvation is by faith not by works of the Law.

Romans 10: Whoever calls on the name of the Lord will be saved.

16. v 1 May our heart's cry be as Paul's – for the salvation of the Jews.
17. v 2 Pray for the ultra orthodox who 'are zealous for God but their zeal is not based on knowledge' and having sought to establish a righteousness of their own, 'they did not submit to God's righteousness' (NIV).
18. v 3-4 For all Israel to see that 'Christ is the goal of the Torah for righteousness to everyone who believes'.
19. v 3-10 Pray for many more in Israel to make the confession that 'Jesus is Lord' and believe in their hearts that He rose from the dead, thereby gaining salvation and righteousness.
20. v 11 Pray for joy and hope to fill those who believe, so it is infectious.

February

21. v 12 There is only one path of salvation for all – through Jesus/Yeshua. Some preach one for Jews and another for Gentiles. Pray for this confusion to stop.
22. v 13-14 Pray for all believers to preach the truth, not water down the gospel to avoid the 'rock of offence', thus leading people astray by being 'seeker-friendly'.
23. v 14-15 Pray for the evangelists now working in Israel, and for more to be raised up.
24. v 16 Pray for God to melt the hard hearts in Israel that He may find faith amongst His people.
25. v 17 For the deaf ears to be unblocked to hear the good news.
26. v 18 For the gospel to go to the ends of Israel and the earth so there are no excuses.
27. v 19 For the Gentile nations, especially the church, to make Israel jealous.
28. v 20-21 For Israel's disobedience and obstinacy to be broken by the love of God.

March

Preservation and Return of God's people

Purim Parade - Photo courtesy Lawrence Hirsch

For if you remain silent at this time, relief and deliverance will arise for the Jews from another place and you and your father's house will perish. And who knows whether you have not attained royalty for such a time as this? Esther 4:14

Do not fear, for I am with you; I will bring your offspring from the east, and gather you from the west. I will say to the north, 'Give them up!' And to the south, 'Do not hold them back.' Bring My sons from afar and My daughters from the ends of the earth. Is 43:5-7

March

This month we focus on aliya – literally meaning 'to go up' or in other words to migrate to Israel. A major prophetic move of God in our time is the re-gathering of the Jewish people from the ends of the earth back to Israel. It began around 1880 and has continued in waves ever since. God promised to bring His people home from their exile in the nations and called the Gentiles to be part of this process. While just over half of the world's Jews now live in Israel, that means we are only 50% of the way there – and God says He will not leave any behind (Ezek 39:25-29).

The Feast of Lots, Purim, generally occurs this month, although it can begin late February. This celebrates the deliverance of the Jews from the hand of Haman. The wicked plot is told in the book of Esther.

Aliya

Countries with the largest Jewish populations:

1. Israel, 6,700,000. 74% of the population of Israel is Jewish. Pray for the Jews who were born there or have returned to stay in Israel and not desire to emigrate. Israel has a glorious future. Is 60:1-9
2. USA, 5,700,000. America has by far the greatest number of Jews who need to move. 90% of these are Ashkenazi (European) Jews. Is 43:5-7
3. France, 465,000. Most of France's Jews are Sephardi (Spanish- speaking) or Mizrahi (Middle Eastern or North African). They are mainly found in Paris, Marseille, Lyon, Strasbourg and Toulouse regions. Jer 32:37-44
4. Canada, 385,000. Most Canadian Jews are found in Ontario, Quebec, British Columbia, Manitoba, and Alberta. They are of Ashkenazi, Sephardi and Mizrahi origin. Ezek 11:14-20

All Israel Shall be Saved

5. Great Britain, 269,500. Britain expelled the Jews in 1290 and only allowed them back in the 1655. Is 49:12-13
6. Argentina, 200,000. Jews arrived there in the 16th century after the Spanish inquisition. Argentine Jews are currently settled in Buenos Aires, Cordoba, Santa Fe, Entre Rios and Tucumán regions. They include Ashkenazi, Sephardic and Mizrahi Jews. Jer 31:16-19
7. Russia, 186,000. Severe persecution (pogroms) reduced the once large population of Russian Jews. Since the Iron Curtain has fallen, several million have migrated to Israel. Jer 23:5-8
8. Australia, 112,500. Melbourne and Sydney have the largest Jewish communities. The first Jews arrived as convicts from Britain. Is 11:11,12
9. Germany, 100,000 Most German Jews were massacred during the Holocaust and those remaining escaped shortly after. Some have been welcomed back since the 1990s but on condition that they never migrate to Israel. Jer 16:14-21
10. Brazil, 95,000. The Brazilian Jewish population is concentrated in the cities of Sao Paulo and Rio de Janeiro. They arrived after the Spanish inquisition or later escaping from Russian pogroms and Nazi persecution. Obadiah v20. The Sepharad in this verse are the Spanish-speaking or Sephardic Jews.
11. South Africa 70,000. Many South African Jews have escaped to Western countries rather than go to Israel. Amos 9:14-15
12. Ukraine 63,000. Before WWI almost one third of Ukraine's population was Jewish. About 70% of them were killed in the Russian wars or during the German occupation. Many have come home to Israel in recent years. Jer 50:4-5

As you can see, 80% of Jewish people living outside Israel live in the US, with the majority living in the major cities. The state of New York has more than 2 million Jews and about 13% of the city of New York's total population is Jewish. It is the largest Jewish centre outside of Israel. Other US cities are Los Angeles (617,480), Miami (527,750), Washington DC – Baltimore area (297,290), Chicago (294,280) and Philadelphia (292,450).

Outside of Israel and the US, the greatest population areas are in Paris,

March

France (250,000-300,000 in 2016 but decreasing rapidly due to anti-Semitism), Toronto, Canada (190,000), London, UK (160,000), Buenos Aires, Argentina (160,000) and Montreal, Canada (90,000).

The Jewish Agency is the department in Israel that organises and coordinates bringing the Jews home. Some other organisations assisting them are: Nefesh B'Nefesh (Jewish), which brings many young people to Israel to give them a taste for the country and entice them to want to migrate; Shavei Israel (Jewish); Ebenezer Operation Exodus (Christian); Christians Care International (Christian); Operation Tarshish (Christian); The Golden Report (Jerry Golden, Messianic believer).

Most of the large Christian organisations with offices in Israel assist also with integration of new immigrants (*olim*) once they arrive in the Land. There are some major obstacles that need prayer to remove.

- Firstly, Jews who believe in Yeshua (Jesus) cannot make aliya as they are considered to have changed their religion and are therefore no longer Jewish – even though they are often more Jewish than before, and they are following a Jewish Messiah! Those with no faith are welcome, but those who believe the Hebrew Scriptures are not. Sad, but true.
- Secondly, along the same lines, some groups, such as many of the Bnei Menashe in north-east India, have had major influence from Christian missionaries in the past and many of them have become believers. In order to emigrate to Israel, they are faced with denying Christ and undergoing 'conversion' back to Judaism or being left behind. Many deny their Lord in order to have better opportunities available in Israel.
- Christian groups assisting with aliya are not allowed to preach the gospel. They can answer questions if asked, and are allowed to give the people an Old Testament but not a New Testament nor Christian literature nor teach anything about Christianity. This applies also to those assisting the new immigrants in the Land. They must sign a document not to 'proselytise'.

All Israel Shall be Saved

Purim – Feast of Lots – The Story of Esther

The festival of Esther, called Purim, occurs normally in March but can begin in late February. The chart of dates is found in the introduction of this book or you can always check the date for each year at https://www.hebcal.com/holidays.

The Scroll or Book of Esther is read in the congregations and the story is celebrated in schools, synagogues and families. It is a fun time as the children dress up in costumes (unfortunately often demonic) and parade through the streets. It is traditional to stamp feet on the ground or make noise to drown out the name of Haman, the villain who plotted to wipe out the Jewish race. The day before the Feast is a fast day to remember that the people were asked to fast for three days (4:16) before Esther risked her life to go before the king. Pray about doing an Esther fast for breakthrough for the salvation of Israel. God heard their cry and delivered them. May He hear ours also.

Ami Ortiz

It is a tradition to send food parcels and gifts to one another and to the poor at Purim. In the town of Ariel, on 20th March, 2008, Ami, son of Messianic pastors David and Leah Ortiz, found one such parcel on their doorstep. As Ami, then aged 15, opened the parcel it exploded showering his body with shrapnel and bringing him to within a whisker of death. He miraculously survived. After two and a half years of excruciating recovery and rehabilitation, dozens of operations and plastic surgeries, and years of spiritual, mental and emotional recovery, Ami is doing well, pursuing his studies in USA and furthering his love for basketball. You can read his story and the ensuing injustices (largely because they are Messianic believers) regarding the arrest and conviction of the perpetrator at https://amiortiz.org. Pray that Ami will not suffer trauma as he celebrates this festival.

March

March Prayer Points – Purim and Aliya

Purim – from the Book of Esther

Please join Israel in reading the book of Esther at this time and consider joining the Esther Fast. Pray for the Jewish people to be encouraged and strengthened in faith as they read the scroll of Esther in the synagogues worldwide at Purim (Esther 8:15-17, 9:22).

1. The story in the book of Esther took place in Persia, today's Iran. Iran is still Israel's greatest threat, with a diabolical hatred of Israel and near-nuclear capability. Pray for God's protection over Israel and for Iran's leaders to bow to the Almighty or be removed (Esther 1:2, 7:2-6).
2. Pray for God to raise up Mordecais who will instil destiny into their children (2:5-7), watch at the gates to warn of danger both spiritual and physical (2:21-23), recognise the opportunity in the disaster and share Mordecai's faith in God (4:1-3,8,13-14).
3. Pray for God's people (including us) to live under different laws and not bow down to the ungodly demands of false leaders, even when they want to use this against us (3:8).
4. Pray for a Mordecai church and an Israel that will have boldness to declare their faith, even when it may cost them their life. Mordecai was not silent about his protest – he loudly wailed in the midst of the city (4:1)! Pray for God's protection over the courageous Mordecais who speak up for God (3:1-6).
5. Pray for us to be available as Esther was and even say, 'If I perish, I perish' (4:16).
6. Pray for Esthers who will be pure before the Lord, ask for wisdom and seek the favour of the King (2:8-10, 13-15), then act with humility and patience, not presumption (5:1-8, 7:1-3).
7. Pray for God to put His chosen ones in strategic positions in government like Esther and Mordecai 'for such a time as this' (4:14). They did not become proud when they were promoted to leadership (6:10-13).
8. Pray for the Hamans' hearts and motives to be revealed so they fall into their own trap (5:9-14, 7:7-10, 8:3,5).

9. Pray for God to send dreams and visions (or sleepless nights) to save His people (6:1-9). God intervened by drawing the king to the annals of history that night. Pray He will remind world leaders of the true history of God's people and miraculously turn situations around in answer to prayer and fasting (4:16).
10. May the nations recognise that God is with the Jews, and they will surely fall before their God (6:13).
11. God has a signet ring for His people Israel. Pray for her to arise to her calling as priests of the Most High God who will rule with Him over the nations (8:1-2).
12. Pray for the message of the good news of salvation through Yeshua to go out to every place where the Jews are living. This must happen before Satan is loosed to bring destruction (8:10).

Prayer for Aliya

13. Pray for God to move on the hearts of Jews in the diaspora, convicting them regarding their Jewish identity and stirring their hearts to cry out to Him to come home without having to be persecuted to spur them to action. Jer 33:3
14. God says He will leave none behind in the diaspora. Those in the West are the most resistant to moving. They can come now with their belongings or God will put a hook in their mouths to draw them later through persecution. Gen 12:1-2, Ezek 39:27-29
15. Pray for the Lord's love and tenderness to draw the youth that Nefesh B'Nefesh brings to Israel so they want to make aliya. May God help them see the signs of impending persecution and to be willing to leave all to move to Israel. Jer 31:3, Ps 34:8, Lk 21: 25-27
16. Pray for young Jews to see Israel as a land of opportunity and the only safe place for them in the future. Pray for them to see the need to return from the West with their wealth to build up the country and for the believers to hear and obey the Shepherd's voice calling them. Is 55:1-11, Ezek 34:11-16

March

17. Pray for Ebenezer Operation Exodus https://www.eoeaspac.org, Christians Care International https://www.christianscare.org and Jerry Golden https://thegoldenreport.net as they assist the Jews to come home. May the love of God shine through them and touch their hearts. Is 49:22, 60:9
18. Pray for Christians to understand God's plan to bring the Jews home and re-form the nation then give them a new heart. Jer 31:8-10, 31-34, Ezek 20:41-44
19. Pray for the Lord to provide the necessary documentation (many documents were destroyed in the Holocaust and true identities were often disguised) and the finances for relocation expenses. Not every Jew in the West is rich and the costs of emigration can be very high. Israel helps those from poorer countries. Lk 3:11
20. Pray for Jews in Muslim countries to be able to escape with their families and belongings. Ezra 8:21-31
21. Pray for the Jewish National Fund (Jewish) as it works to prepare the infra-structure (especially water infrastructure) for the return of the people. Ps 90:17.
22. The Jewish Agency (Jewish) is the chief body working to bring the Jews home. May they treat their brothers and sisters with great compassion. Ps 102:13
23. Pray for the government to be lenient on those who want to return to Israel (especially the Messianic Jews), and not put obstacles in their way. Is 40:3-5
24. Pray for the new immigrants to be welcomed, be able to learn the language, cope with cultural change and find suitable employment quickly. Lev 19:33-34
25. Pray for the children starting at school to settle in quickly and find friends, especially those who are trying to learn the language. Many new immigrants, especially those from communist countries, have no idea of what the Bible says. Some have never heard of Moses and never had a Passover meal. Prov 22:6-7, Ex 12:14,24
26. God is not bringing His people home to have a secular nation. Pray for the congregations to reach out to the newcomers, help them adjust, build good relationships and preach the gospel in love. Prov 17:17, Matt 22:36-40, 2 Cor 2:14-16

27. Pray for the politicians to understand that they cannot give away the land as it will be needed for another 6-7 million Jews who have yet to come home. Lev 25:23
28. Pray for Christian fishermen to go out to the countries and cities where Jews are residing in the diaspora, find the Jews and encourage them to come home. Jer 16:14-16
29. Pray for those who are sick or elderly to be strong enough to travel, especially from poor countries, as there are much better medical facilities in Israel. Jer 31:10-14, 33:6-7
30. Pray for people not to be deterred by the challenges in Israel of rockets and attacks from hostile neighbours. Is 43:1-7, Jer 33:10-16
31. Pray for Christian organisations assisting with aliya or the absorption process to be asked many questions by their recipients. They are allowed to answer these but not initiate conversations about Christianity. 2 Tim 4:1-2

April

First Fruits of Redemption

The blood shall be a sign for you on the houses where you live; and when I see the blood I will pass over you, and no plague will befall you to destroy you when I strike the land of Egypt. Ex 12:13

...For Christ our Passover has been sacrificed. 1 Cor 5:7

(Jesus Christ) was declared the Son of God with power by the resurrection from the dead... Rom 1:4

But now Christ has been raised from the dead, the first fruits of those who are asleep. 1 Cor 15:20

April

The Spring Feasts – Passover

April is normally the season of the Spring Festivals in Israel, although Passover may begin in late March. Passover (Pesach) is the first of the biblical festivals, beginning on the 14th day of the first month, called Nisan. It is immediately followed by the Feast of Unleavened Bread. These two festivals are now combined into one in most Jewish circles. Passover recalls the story of the exodus - the hard labour in Egypt, the plagues, the Passover lamb and their dramatic escape through the Red (in Hebrew, Reed) Sea. God commanded the Israelites to take one unblemished lamb per household, to kill it at twilight on the 14th day of the first month and place some of the blood on the doorposts and lintel of their house (Ex 12:5-7). They were to eat the lamb with unleavened bread and bitter herbs that same evening, dressed ready to leave in a hurry (Ex 12:8-11). God's promise was that when the Lord passed over the land that night and saw the blood, He would not allow the destroyer to smite them as it did the first sons of the Egyptians (Ex 12:13,23). This festival was to be celebrated on an annual basis to pass the story from generation to generation and to remember the great deliverance of the Lord (Ex 12:14, 24-27).

Passover is a family festival and the story is told around a festive meal, called a 'Seder', eaten in the home, using a special order of service called the Haggadah (re-telling). Some of the prayers go back thousands of years and some of the traditions are more modern, but in many ways, the Haggadah foreshadows the Messiah and tells of His redeeming work. Jesus' last meal was a Passover meal through which He revealed Himself in the bread and the wine. This feast is a wonderful opportunity to relate to your Jewish friends and share Messiah with them, and to pray for God to reveal Himself again as the Jewish people celebrate Passover. It is also an important way of teaching Christians about the Jewish roots of Christianity.

All Israel Shall be Saved

Modern Tradition

A 'Seder' plate is placed in the centre of the table, which contains visual symbols of the Passover story – bitter herbs (horseradish, representing the hard life), lamb shank bone (the sacrificial lamb), parsley or lettuce (like the hyssop used to apply the blood), haroseth (a mixture of apple, nuts, cinnamon and wine, representing the 'mud' for the bricks) and a roasted egg (supposedly remembering the burnt temple). As well as this, there is unleavened bread and four cups of wine, which Jesus used as symbols for His upcoming death. The service concludes with the singing of the 'Hallel' psalms, Psalms 113-118, which is most likely what Jesus sang just before He went into the Garden of Gethsemane.

Jesus in the Passover

The 'matzah' or unleavened bread used today is square and like a dry biscuit. It has holes vertically and horizontally and reminds us that Jesus was *pierced for our transgressions…by His stripes we are healed* (Is 53:5). Perhaps the most fascinating part of the entire Passover Haggadah, is the mystery of the 'Afikomen'. Before the meal, three matzot (plural of matzah) are wrapped in a special pocket placed on the table. During the meal, the middle matzah is removed, broken in two and one half is hidden, which the children have to find later in the ceremony. 'Afikomen' is a Greek word meaning 'He came'! For Messianic Jews, the three matzot represent the Father, the Son and the Holy Spirit. The middle one is broken (died), wrapped (buried), hidden, then revealed before the third cup of wine (cup of redemption) is drunk. This so clearly speaks of the Messiah Yeshua.

Another tradition is that an extra place is always set at the table with a special cup for Elijah. Towards the end of the service, the children are sent to the door to see if Elijah is coming. This is associated with the prophecy of Malachi:

Behold, I am going to send Elijah the prophet before the coming of the great and terrible day of the Lord. Mal 4:5

April

Passover brings with it a tremendous expectation of the coming of Messiah for the Jewish people, as well as a remembrance of past deliverance. For Messianic Jews, as Peter said:

The things which God announced beforehand by the mouth of all the prophets, that the Christ should suffer, He has thus fulfilled. Acts 3:18

The roots of our communion service lie in this final Passover meal when He instituted the Lord's Supper (Mk 14:12-26). He gave the bread and wine eaten at the festival a new meaning, as they were to represent His body and blood which were soon to be broken and poured out. It was to be a reminder of His death (1 Cor 11:23-26). Jesus, the unblemished Lamb of God (Jn 1:29), was sacrificed for our sins at Passover time so that when His blood is applied to the doorposts and lintels of our hearts, the destroyer (Satan) has no claim to bring death on us. Jesus has become our Passover Lamb (1 Cor 5:7). Hallelujah!

The Feast of Unleavened Bread

The Feast of Unleavened Bread (Hag HaMatzot) is associated with Passover and follows immediately after it, starting on 15 Nisan, for seven days (Lev 23:6-8, Num 28:17-25). As no leaven (yeast or other ferment) was to be eaten or even found in the house during this time (Ex 12:15-20, Dt 16:3-4), observant Jews will do a total house clean before Passover, removing every speck of dust from the house and scrubbing every surface. Shops in Israel cover over all foods that contain yeast, and ordinary bread is almost impossible to find unless you travel to an Arab area.

Rabbi Yeshua referred to leaven as a symbol for evil or sinful teachings or practices (Matt 16:6,11-12, Lk 12:1). He has done away with sin once for all.

...He has been manifested to put away sin by the sacrifice of Himself ...By this will we have been sanctified through the offering of the body of Jesus Christ once for all...For by one offering, He has perfected for all time those who are sanctified (Heb 9:26, 10:10,14).

Feast of the First Fruits

The third holy convocation, First Fruits is commanded in Lev 23:10-14 and began what the Jews called the 'counting of the Omer' (a measure of grain). On the first day after the Sabbath holiday, normally 16 Nisan, the priests would wave a sheaf of barley before the Lord in the temple. The instructions and prayer to be offered in the temple are recorded in Deut 26:1-11. There was a special barley field cultivated on the opposite side of the Kidron Valley for the first fruits sacrifice for the nation. The barley was taken from there on the evening of Nisan 15. Three members of the Sanhedrin went to this field to harvest the first sheaves and bring them to the Temple, where they were threshed, parched over fire, winnowed and milled into fine flour to be presented the following morning as the national first fruits offering. Today this offering is not made as there is no temple but the counting of the omer is still carried out.

Jesus, the First Fruit

Early in the morning of the third day, 16 Nisan (or the day after the Sabbath – some say 17 Nisan), as this first fruits offering was being brought into the Temple, Jesus was being raised from the dead, as the *first fruits of those who are asleep* (1 Cor 15:20)! His body had been taken from across the Kidron at the Garden of Gethsemane, threshed by Roman soldiers, but was now raised incorruptible, as a fine first-fruits offering to the Father and an assurance that *death is swallowed up in victory* (1 Cor 15:54, Is 25:8). Jesus' resurrection, as the first fruits offering, is the certainty that we also who believe will rise from the dead to eternal life in imperishable bodies (1 Cor 15:52), and the wicked shall face the fire of God (Rev 20:11-15).

Jesus' Last Week

There are three Passovers mentioned in the gospels, which lead scholars to calculate Jesus' ministry as about 3½ years long. His final days in Jerusalem were at Passover time. There were different calendars operating in the first century – it is known that the Essenes had their own one that differed from

April

the Rabbinic one used in the Temple. It is therefore possible for Jesus to have had an early Passover meal and to have been crucified at *exactly* the same hour as the lambs were being sacrificed in the Temple on the following day! There is much dispute over these dates, but the following is one possibility. Others say that He rose on 16 Nisan. Remember that Hebrew days begin and end at sunset, not midnight.

Date	OT event	NT event
Nissan 10	Unblemished lamb chosen Ex 12:3	Jesus rides into Jerusalem on a donkey, cleanses temple Matt 21:1-11
Nissan 11	Lamb inspected for imperfection	Fig tree cursed. Teaching in Temple. Inspected by rabbis who could find no fault. Matt 21:18-27, 22:15-46, Lk 19:47-48
Nissan 12		Olivet discourse Matt 24:3-25:46
Nissan 13		Mary anoints Jesus' feet. Matt 26:6-13, Mk 14:3-9, Jn 12:1-7. Disciples prepare for Passover in the day time. Matt 26:17-19, Lk 22:7-13. Last Supper in the evening. Matt 26:20-30
Nissan 14	Lamb slain at 3 pm High Priest declares 'It is finished.' Passover meal after sundown Ex 12:6-8	Arrested at night Matt 26:20-27:56. Crucified 9 am, died 3 pm and buried before High Sabbath begins. Jn 19:31
Nissan 15	Passover possibly held by Rabbis on 15 Nisan in the 1st century.	In the grave. Guard set. Matt 27:62-66.
Nissan 16		In the grave. Sabbath
Nissan 17	First fruits brought to Temple. Lev 23:10	Before sunrise Resurrection Matt 28:1-10, 1 Cor 15:20-27.

All Israel Shall be Saved

At the death of Jesus, the veil in the temple was torn and we can enter into His holy place (Matt 27:51-53). After the resurrection, He appeared to Mary and the other women (Matt 28:8-10), the disciples on the Emmaus road (Lk 24:13-35), the disciples in Jerusalem (Lk 24:36-49, Jn 20:19-23), the disciples with Thomas (Jn 20:26-29), Peter and the disciples in Galilee (Jn 21:1-17, Matt 28:16-20), and more than 500 people at once (1 Cor 15:6). We can rejoice for He is alive, and has overcome death (1 Cor 15:54-57).

April Prayer Points - Passover/Unleavened Bread/ First Fruits

1. Praise God that the Jewish people have faithfully kept Passover all their generations. Ex 12:42
2. Praise God that He is the same yesterday, today and forever. He delivered the Israelites out of Egypt with a mighty hand and He can deliver them today from the hand of their enemies. Jud 6:8-9
3. In these days of unleavened bread, let's make sure are hearts are clean. 1 Cor 5:6-8, 1 Jn 1:8-10. As the Jews prepare for Passover they do a thorough house clean. Pray that they will do the same spiritually. Ps 24:2-5, Ps 51:1-4
4. Declare I will bring you out from under the yoke of the Egyptians. Praise God that He did that. Ex 6:6-7
5. I will free you from being slaves (Ex 6:6). As they celebrate the days of their freedom, may they know God's deliverance from the slavery of sin. Thank the Lord for our freedom and pray that Israel will realise that they need freeing from the bonds of sin and death and come into life in Jesus. Rom 8:1-2, 7:22-25
6. I will redeem you with an outstretched arm and mighty acts of judgement (Ex 6:6). Thank the Lord for this promise. May the Redeemer rise up and encompass His people and judge their enemies. Is 54:8
7. I will take you as my own people and I will be your God (Ex 6:7). This is a marriage covenant. Pray for the bride of Christ to be aroused with love for her Bridegroom. Is 62:5
8. For Israel to know that Yahweh is the Lord their God (Ex 6:7). Deut 4:34-35

April

9. I will bring you into the land (Ex 6:8). Pray for God to stir the hearts of those Jews still living in the US, Europe and Australia to move to Israel. Is 43:5-7
10. I will give it to you as a possession (Ex 6:8). Pray for Israel to acknowledge that the land belongs to God and he has given it to them as their inheritance and not to swap land for a false hope of peace. Lev 25:23
11. Unleavened bread is the bread of affliction. Pray for Israel to know that Yeshua was afflicted for them. Is 53:4,7
12. The matzah is pierced and striped. Pray that as the Jewish people eat the matzah they will see that Jesus was pierced for our transgression, and by His stripes we are healed. Is 53:5
13. Pray that we may receive fresh manna from the Lord today. Ex 16:14-16
14. Pray for Israel to beware of the leaven of the Pharisees – religion not relationship with God. Matt 16:11-12
15. Judgement came upon the gods of Egypt, especially the sons of Egypt for killing the sons of the Hebrews at birth. Repent for the plague of abortion that is taking place in Israel and the Western world. Jer 32:3
16. Pray for the fear of God to fall on the nations surrounding Israel once again because they see that God is with His people. Josh 2:8-11
17. Pray for Israel to remember what it is like being slaves and not treat others harshly. Ex 23:9
18. Pray for God to part the waters for His people again as the nations try to close in on Israel politically and divide up her land. Joel 3:1-2
19. In the Passover service the middle one of three matzot is broken and hidden for a time, then revealed. Pray that the people will see this as a symbol of the Son of God who was broken and has been hidden in Heaven for a time, but will shortly be revealed. Jn 14:2-6
20. Pray for the revelation for Israel that the Passover Lamb has been slain. 1 Cor 5:7, Jn 1:29
21. Pray for an awareness that only by the shedding of blood can sin be forgiven. Heb 9:22, Lev 17:11
22. Prophetically put the blood of Jesus over the doorposts of the nation at this vulnerable time so the angel of death cannot come to destroy. Ps 41:1-2

All Israel Shall be Saved

23. The third cup of the four Passover cups is the cup of redemption, at which time Jesus instituted the Holy Communion. He declared the New Covenant, written on our hearts. Pray for God to give His people a new heart and write this covenant on their hearts this Passover. Jer 31:33-34
24. This is my body given for you. Jesus is the bread of life. Let Israel come and partake of the bread that satisfies and believe on the Lord so they will not be thirsty. 1 Cor 11:23-24, Jn 6:35.
25. The cup is the New Covenant in His blood. Pray for Israel to embrace the covenant cut in the blood of Messiah. Lk 22:20
26. The cup of Elijah reminds us that Elijah must come before the Messiah to prepare the way. Pray for the Jews to recognise that John the Baptist has fulfilled this. Mal 4:5-6
27. For those still in the diaspora who pray 'Next Year in Jerusalem' at the end of the Passover to be stirred to make it a reality. Is 43:5-7, Jer 32:37, Hos 11:10-11
28. May an Elijah generation of young people be raised up that will turn the hearts of the fathers to the children and the children's hearts to their fathers to heal the land and the generational gap and preach the message of repentance. Mal 4:6, Matt 3:1-12
29. Pray for an expectation to arise that Messiah is coming soon. Jn 16:22, Matt 24:29-31
30. Following Passover comes the festival of first fruits – the resurrection day. Rejoice that Jesus is risen as the first fruits of those that are asleep. Hallelujah! 1 Cor 15:20-22

May

Rebirth of a Nation in a Day

Wheat field ripe for harvest

But you will receive power when the Holy Spirit has come upon you; and you shall be My witnesses both in Jerusalem, and in all Judea and Samaria, and even to the remotest part of the earth. Acts 1:8

Can a country be born in a day or a nation be brought forth in a moment? Yet no sooner is Zion in labor than she gives birth to her children. Is 66:8b, c (NIV)

Then He said to His disciples, 'The harvest is plentiful, but the workers are few. Therefore pray to the Lord of the harvest that He may send out workers into His harvest field.' Matt 9:37-38 (Tree of Life Version)

May

In April-May, Israel celebrates Independence Day (5 Iyar) but the day immediately preceding is their Memorial Day for the soldiers who sacrificed their lives in defending the land. The 28th of the month of Iyar is Jerusalem Day, remembering the victory of the Six Day War when Jerusalem was re-united under Israeli control. Shavuot/Pentecost is on 6 Sivan, which falls in late May or early June.

The Beginning of the Nation

Israel's legitimacy comes essentially from God Himself. He owns the Land (Lev 25:23, Ezek 36:5, Joel 3:2). He has chosen the Hebrew people as His own possession and given the land of Canaan as their inheritance forever (Gen 17:7-8). He has chosen Jerusalem as His earthly dwelling place (1 Kg 11:36, Ps 132:13). Anyone who tries to take the land will come up against the Landowner Himself (Joel 3:2, Ezek chapter 35)!

Satan wants to rule the earth and through the ages has used many different people groups to try to disrupt God's plans and annihilate the Jewish people – Assyrians, Persians, Babylonians, Greeks, Romans, Crusaders, Spaniards, Islam, Russians, Hitler, Iran and the UN to name a few. He is unlikely to give up before Jesus comes and he is chained and thrown into the abyss for 1000 years (Rev 20:1-3). We need to be careful whose side we are on because quite a few of these persecutors did so under the banner of Christ.

During Israel's exile amongst the nations, many different people groups lived in the land but none made it their capital – Romans (70-324 CE), Byzantine Christians (324-638), early Muslims (638-1099), Crusader Christians (1099-1187), Ayyubid Muslims (1187-1259), Mamluk Muslims (1250-1516), Ottoman Muslims (1516-1917), British (1917-1948). Only since Jerusalem was returned to Jewish hands in 1967 has it become a 'holy' site for Islam. Prior to that, Mecca and Medina were the pilgrim destinations.

All Israel Shall be Saved

1917 – WWI Balfour Declaration and ANZAC Military Breakthrough

Jews have never completely left the land, and numbers returned after the Spanish inquisition, mainly living in four cities – Jerusalem, Safed, Tiberias and Hebron. Around 1880, the modern influx began because of pogroms (ethnic cleansing) in various countries. The land was under Ottoman rule until 1917, when the British Army and their allies drove them out.

Charge of Beersheba 1917

The first breakthrough in WWI in Palestine came on 31 October, 1917, when British, Australian and New Zealand Forces captured Beersheba after a dramatic, courageous charge of the Light Horsemen an hour before sunset. This occurred the same day as the British War Cabinet decided to allow a Jewish homeland in their ancient land, which was put in writing as the Balfour Declaration. The war continued for another year until the Ottomans were pushed right back to the area of modern-day Turkey. The physical and legal breakthroughs cleared the way for the return of the Jewish people on a larger scale, albeit through many difficulties as Britain reneged on her mandated promises.

1920 – San Remo – The League of Nations

After World War I, the Ottoman Empire was partitioned into various mandates – the French were to administer Syria, which became Syria and Lebanon, and the British were given the mandate for Palestine and Mesopotamia, which became Iraq, Jordan and Israel. The San Remo Agreement, passed at San Remo, Italy, on 25 April, 1920, was based on the Balfour Declaration and Article 22 of the League of Nations Covenant and the mandates given lasted until the lands became self-sufficient enough to govern themselves. This was the first legally binding legitimacy for the State of Israel and it has never been revoked, though buried and forgotten by most of the world. It was confirmed unanimously by all 51 nations (including Arab nations) of

May

the League of Nations and ratified on 24 July, 1922. The Republic of Turkey emerged in 1923. The Kingdom of Iraq was formed in 1932, the Lebanese Republic became independent in 1943 and the Syrian Arab Republic and Hashemite Kingdom of Jordan both followed in 1946. Last of all was the State of Israel in 1948. If Israel has no legitimacy, neither does Syria, Lebanon, Jordan, or Iraq as they are all based on the same legal agreement.

The British Mandate for Palestine was to provide a homeland for both the Jews and the Arabs who resided in the area called Palestine. Palestinians were simply residents of Palestine, whatever their ethnic or religious allegiance.

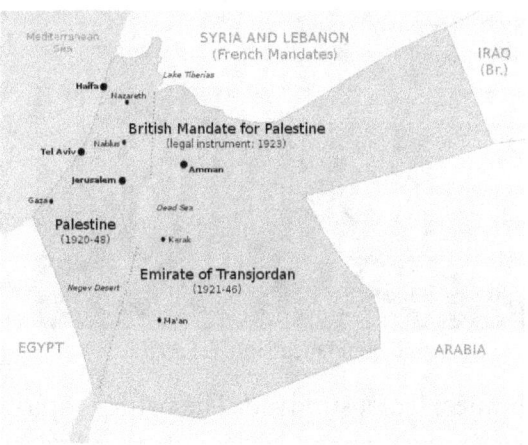

The British soon reneged on their promises to the Jews, due to Arab pressure, and carved off 77% of Palestine for the Arabs, dividing Palestine at the Jordan River. Jews were not allowed to settle there. This was re-named Transjordan in 1922 and later became the Hashemite Kingdom of Jordan in 1946, cleverly disguising its name, since 136 CE, Palestine.

The remaining 23% of Palestine was given to the Jewish people, which is less than 1/3 the size of Tasmania. However, Jews *and* Arabs were allowed to settle in this area west of the Jordan River, which they did, altering the demographics. However, this division largely agreed with the rightful inheritance God has given to the Arab peoples to the east of the land He gave Israel (Deut 2:4-5, 9,19).

1947 – United Nations

After WWII and the murder of six million Jewish people in the concentration camps of Europe, on 29 November, 1947, the United Nations General Assembly adopted Resolution 181 (11), with 33 votes for, 13 against and 10 abstentions, recommending the creation of independent Arab and Jewish

States and a special International Regime for the city of Jerusalem. This again legalised Israel to become a nation. However, the boundaries were not in accordance with God's Word, slicing more land off the 23% that Israel had been left following Britain's earlier partition. Israel agreed to the diminished land, but the Muslim nations did not. The UN had conveniently ignored the San Remo Agreement and also forgotten that the whole of Jordan had already been given to the Palestinian Arabs!

1948 – Declaration of Statehood

Independance Hall Tel Aviv

The State of Israel was declared by David Ben Gurion on 14 May, 1948, just before the Sabbath began, to come into effect at midnight when the British departed. All the surrounding nations of Egypt, Jordan, Syria, Lebanon and Iraq, immediately went to war to 'wipe Israel off the map'. Against all odds, pitted against five established armies, Israel survived. The battle is spiritual, not political. Islam can never accept that it can lose land that was once conquered by Islam. That would mean that someone is stronger than Allah, and he demands that jihad be waged to restore 'face' (honour). Thus peace in Islam means that Islam must rule and dominate while the conquered people must be in subjection. This spiritual force does not accept equality and a ceasefire is only acceptable when the Muslim people are weak and then only until they are again strong enough to continue jihad. This is the sad reality of living in a Muslim-majority Middle East. But God has stood by His people in every war they have fought – and they continue to stand, by His grace and because of His covenant.

Israeli Politics – The Knesset

The Israeli government is called the Knesset (assembly), and its name derives from the great assembly held by Ezra and Nehemiah in the 5th century BCE. There are 120 members represented by different parties that form a coalition for a four-year term. The political system is a democracy and in elections, citizens over 18 years of age vote for a party rather than an individual. The whole country is one district. To have a seat in parliament, a party must gain 3.25% of the vote. Parties have proportional representation so if they get 5% of the vote, they will have six members in the Knesset (i.e. 5% of 120 seats). The President offers the leader of the party that has the highest percentage of votes the first chance to form a government, but since 1949 no single party has been able to achieve the 61 seats needed. Thus, there are coalitions formed on agreed terms. If no one can get

enough agreement to form government, a new election is called. Thus Israel had three elections in a year in 2019-2020. There is a wide range of views within the Knesset as it includes ultra-orthodox Jewish parties, centre parties, 'settler' parties, left wing parties and Arab parties. Benjamin Netanyahu is Israel's longest- serving Prime Minister and his right-wing party is called 'Likud' meaning 'consolidation'.

Shavuot – Feast of Weeks – Pentecost

Shavuot (meaning weeks) occurs in late spring or early summer. It takes place 50 days after Passover, and is called Pentecost (50th) in Greek. Agriculturally, it celebrates the harvest of the grains – wheat and barley. In the Temple, two loaves of wheat bread were waved before the Lord, together with the animal sacrifices (Lev 23:15-21, Num 28:26-31, Deut 16:9-12). It was to be a feast of rejoicing and remembering that they had been brought out of slavery into freedom. It was a thank offering for the grain harvest, the first fruits of which belong to the Lord.

As the Temple is no longer standing, the offerings cannot be offered, but the rabbis have associated Shavuot with the giving of the Law on Mt Sinai because that occurred in the third month after they left Egypt (Ex 19:1). It is traditional to eat dairy foods at Shavuot. The readings in the synagogues at this time are the Book of Ruth (because she came to Bethlehem at this time of year) and also Ezek 1:1-28, 3:12 and Hab 2:20-3:19. These tell of a vision of the throne and glory of God in His heavenly Temple surrounded by fire and wind.

In about 30 CE, as the priests and faithful Jews came to the Temple to bring their sheaves of wheat as a first fruits thanksgiving to the Lord for a bountiful grain harvest to come, the Holy Spirit fell on the apostles in the upper room. Wind, fire and the glory of God were manifest in Jerusalem that day, as this Scripture was being read in the Temple. Men of fear were turned into bold ambassadors for Christ and began preaching the message of Jesus the Messiah, who had just fulfilled the prophecies of the Old Covenant. What's more, they told it in many languages they could not speak, and were understood by the Jews gathered in the Temple from many different countries, who were celebrating this second pilgrimage festival. The supernatural Holy Spirit of God empowered them to continue the work of Jesus on earth and spread the good news of salvation throughout the world (Acts chapter 2).

As the Law in stone was given on Mt Sinai, 3,000 people died because of idolatry (Ex 32:28). On this first Shavuot after Yeshua's death and resurrection, a new law was written on the hearts of 3,000 believers and a harvest of Jews found salvation in His name (Acts 2:41). A new covenant was established – the church was born and a new era had begun.

I will put My law within them and on their heart I will write it; and I will be their God and they shall be My people. Jer 31:33

How awesome that God would command His people to make a pilgrimage to Jerusalem to witness first-hand the fulfilment of these prophetic Spring festivals – the sacrificial lamb slain on the cross for our sin, His resurrection as the first fruit from the dead, and the outpouring of the Holy Spirit and birth of the church as the first fruit of salvation. And these all occurred on

May

the exact day on the biblical calendar that God had established in Leviticus chapter 23. Has God then established a precedent for the later Fall festivals as well? We shall see later.

May Prayer Points – Shavuot and Government

1. He is the God who comes in fire, at the sound of the shofar, with earthquakes and a voice of thunder. Pray for the fire of the Holy Spirit to fall on Israel. Ex 19:18-19
2. Reflect on the 10 Commandments today. Pray for these to be the basis of Israel's government and legal system. Ex 20:1-18
3. Pray for these to be restored to our Western government, schools and law courts. Deut 6:1-9
4. Pray for the believers to wait on the power from on high before moving. Lk 24:49
5. Pray for the believers to be in unity awaiting God's outpouring of His Spirit once again. Acts 1:14
6. Pray for the believers to realise what power is available to us and wisely use this. Acts 2:1-13
7. Pray for revelations to the Jews such as in John 21:1-11.
8. Pray for the Lord to converse with His people as on the Emmaus road and open the Scriptures to them. Luke 24:13-35
9. Pray for the believers to take the great commission seriously. Matt 28:16-20
10. Pray for the Holy Spirit to fill His people with power to witness. Acts 1:8
11. Pray for the gospel of the Kingdom to be preached, not just the gospel of salvation. Acts 1:3
12. Pray for the gift of prophecy to be released with dreams and visions on young and old. Acts 2:17-18
13. Pray for the believers to recognise the signs of our times. Acts 2:19-21.
14. Pray for us to prepare and be ready for the end-time harvest to come in. Acts 2:41
15. Pray for all government ministers to humble themselves and acknowledge God as the rightful King of their country and choose to follow Him. Is 33:22, Is 66:2, 1 Pet 5:6-7

16. Pray for God to be honoured by Israel's parliamentarians so Israel can indeed be a 'light to the nations'. 1 Sam 2:30, Is 42:6
17. Pray for wisdom for all Members of the Knesset to be directed by the Lord to lead the country. Prov 21:1
18. Pray for unified and stable government. Pray for a willingness for all parties to compromise for the sake of the country and for unity and cooperation between the factions. Phil 2:2
19. Pray for no leader to give away land or divide Jerusalem for an elusive and non-genuine 'peace' (Ezek 13:9-10, Is 28:14-18). There are still six million or more Jews to come home and the land is needed to accommodate these. Pray instead for the infrastructure and housing to prepare for the influx of Jews making aliya in the coming years. Ezek 36:33-36.
20. Pray for government policies and coalition partnerships to reflect God's righteousness, not push individual, human, ungodly agendas. Ps 94:11-12
21. Pray for a firm stand against UN pressure, the right words when dealing with the media and for the media to communicate this clearly to the world. Ps 35:20, Ps 37:30
22. Pray for the religious spirit in the ultra-orthodox controlled Religious Affairs Department to be bound, to miraculously open doors for Messianic evangelism (1 Cor 16:9). They must welcome Yeshua before He will return. Matt 23:39
23. Pray for the ultra-orthodox grip on immigration (which discriminates against Messianic believers) to be loosened. For God's favour for visas for Christians working in the land and Messianic Jews seeking citizenship. Ex 34:9
24. Pray for the Minister for Defence to have God's strategic wisdom in decisions regarding defence (Prov 3:5-7, 2 Sam 5:19, 23). Pray for the issue of the ultra-orthodox exemption from serving in the army to be resolved or compromised and not cause a stalemate in government.
25. Pray for Israel's economy to remain strong and based on God's economic system. Pray for prosperity as they develop the new oil and gas fields in the sea. Jer 29:11, Lk 6:38, Deut 30:8-9
26. Pray for God to heal the land, cause the desert to blossom (Isaiah chapter 35), cause the crops to bear fruit 100-fold (Hos 2:21-23) and for creative ways to protect Israel's fragile and varied environment. Gen 2:15

May

27. Pray that the children will learn God's Word (not rabbinical myths) and for God to plant His truth in the hearts of the people. Ps 119:160
28. Pray for the Lord to continue to give His people innovative, creative and groundbreaking ideas in IT, medicine and science. Gen 1:26-27
29. Pray for a just and fair social security system for the needy and jobs for the able (Zech 7:9-10). Pray for a Biblical Kingdom culture that honours traditional marriage, and stands against pornography, child abuse and sexual sins. Gen 1:27-28, 2:22-24
30. Pray for Christian tourism to continue to flourish. Mic 4:2, Zech 8:20-23
31. Pray for Israel's law to be based on the Bible not on humanism or the world's (Babylonian) system. Ps 89:14

June

Defending God's Purposes

Photo Courtesy Lawrence Hirsch

The LORD is my light and my salvation; whom shall I fear? The LORD is the defense of my life; Whom shall I dread?...For in the day of trouble He will conceal me in His tabernacle... He will lift me up on a rock. And now my head will be lifted up above my enemies around me, and I will offer in His tent sacrifices with shouts of joy... Ps 27:1, 5-6

My help comes from the LORD, who made heaven and earth. He will not allow your foot to slip; He who keeps you will not slumber. Behold, He who keeps Israel will neither slumber nor sleep...The LORD will protect you from all evil...The LORD will guard your going out and your coming in from this time forth and forever. Ps 121:2-4, 7-8

June

The birthing of a nation in the midst of hostile neighbours dominated by a religious spirit, which considers any territory taken from it as unacceptable and demands jihad for its return, is no easy matter. Hence, Israel has had to face eight wars since its inception in 1948, plus numerous uprisings and constant armed conflict from the north and the south, and in many cases also from within. Our focus this month is for those who defend the land and its people.

1948 War of Independence. When the British withdrew from its mandate over Palestine (which included today's Jordan), Israel declared its statehood and a nation was born in a day on 14 May (Is 66:8), just before the Sabbath began. Immediately, it was involved in the War of Independence as armies from Egypt, Jordan, Syria, Lebanon and Iraq set out to destroy the fledgling nation. Against all odds, Israel survived and the Arabs displaced by this conflict (who had been told by their leaders to temporarily flee until they wiped Israel out) unfortunately ended up in refugee camps. At the same time, Jews from many Muslim nations were forced to flee their homes and escape with nothing. There were about 600,000 people on both sides who were displaced. Israel absorbed the Jews but the Arab refugees were kept as political pawns rather than being absorbed. This continues to this day.

1967 Six-Day War. Syria attacked Israel over the Golan Heights and Egypt and Jordan joined in. In six days, Israel had an overwhelming victory that wiped out the Egyptian air force before it took off, drove Syria from the Golan, captured the Sinai from Egypt and returned the Temple Mount and Jerusalem to Israel.

1973 Yom Kippur War. Egypt and Syria attacked Israel on its holiest day of Yom Kippur (Day of Atonement). Despite early heavy losses, Israel managed to win the advantage and eventually a cease-fire was agreed and in 1979, a peace agreement with Egypt was established that has held to this day.

Rabbi Goren at Western wall 1967

All Israel Shall be Saved

1982 The PLO lost their headquarters in the 'West Bank' in 1967 and moved to Jordan where they caused so much trouble with their violence that they were evicted in 1970 and they moved to Southern Lebanon. In 1982, Israel entered Lebanon to deal with PLO strongholds.

2006 Hezbollah attacked Israel and captured a number of soldiers. Israel retaliated, entering Lebanon and attacking Hezbollah strongholds.

As well as these, there have been other conflicts involving Egypt and the Suez in 1956, the Gaza War (2008-2009) and Operation Pillar of Defense (2012) and Protective Edge (2014) into Gaza to deal with Hamas.

The Israeli Defense Force (IDF)

The IDF includes the army, navy and air force. It was established in May 1948 after the state was declared, formed from the Hagganah (Defence) that had been functioning since 1920 to defend the land and people from attacks. Jewish forces – the Zion Mule Corps and the Jewish Legion – had served as part of the British forces in WWI, with the latter being the first Jewish group to defend their territory in modern times.

The IDF has a regular army, a permanent army and a reserve army. The permanent members are those who have chosen this as a profession, and the reserves serve for one month every three years until they turn 40 (45 for officers), and can be called up in case of war. The IDF is a conscription army and men normally serve for three years and women for two years of compulsory service, although they may choose to do an additional year.

They can enter from 17 years of age but are conscripted at 18. There are also 'national service' volunteers who can serve in non-combative roles and Jewish recruits from overseas who serve. Arab citizens are not conscripted

June

but may choose to join. The Druze sect sends its sons to the Israeli army. Many Christian Arab citizens also serve their country. The ultra-orthodox may serve but most are exempted and not encouraged by their community in order to protect their insular lifestyle. This has been a divisive issue in the Israeli community and political scene.

Unfortunately, Israel has to spend a large amount of its budget on defence – over 5% but this is decreasing as reliance on cyber intelligence and advanced weaponry replaces warfare on the ground in many cases. It has had to respond to new challenges such as combating underground tunnels and incendiary balloons in the sky.

Concerns

- The IDF has a huge problem with abortion. With all the young ladies being in the military and lax, Western sexual practices being common, pregnancy is not something that the IDF wants while women are in compulsory service. Girls are offered two free abortions and should they not accept, pregnant women are discharged from the army, so much pressure is applied. It is astounding that many rabbis generally endorse abortion. While protecting life on the ground, the army is destroying life in the womb!

There are 40,000 abortions each year in Israel and 9% of all pregnancies end in abortion. They are mostly government subsidised and the baby is legally not considered a person until it is disconnected from the umbilical cord.

- Young believers are thrown into a very secular environment in the army. They have little time to come aside, pray and read their Bibles, are in close quarters with others who do not share their biblical values and are sometimes mocked for their beliefs. It is hard for them to stand against the crowd. Pray for them to be strong and grow in their faith, not choose the wide path or hide their faith.

- There are many soldiers who have no families to go home to on the weekend for various reasons – some are from overseas, some are orphans or some have families who are away. There are several Messianic and at least one Arab Christian ministry assisting these lone soldiers by welcoming them to a Shabbat meal.

- Young people are often faced with high levels of responsibility at a young age and see confronting sights they would not choose. One 21-year-old young Messianic officer had 200 soldiers under him during the Lebanon war. Their task was to go in before the foot soldiers and clear out any bombs. They all survived! Pray for them to make wise choices even when these must be instantaneous.

- Many soldiers suffer mental problems if they are confronted with difficult situations during their service, such as injury, accidents, death of a colleague, having to shoot someone to save others from harm or any number of gruesome scenes that war can throw at people. There is at least one Messianic ministry trying to help heal and also prepare young people before they begin their service.

- *The Jewish and Israel Prayer Focus* has a program to pray daily for a Messianic or Christian Arab Israeli soldier during their service. You are not able to communicate with them directly, and in most cases, the pastors or organisations supporting them cannot give a lot of detail because of security issues, but you will have a first name and any information we can provide. If you would like to join our prayer program send a request through our website http://jewishandisraelprayerfocus.org or contact watchmen777@optusnet.com.au.

Yedidya Centre – Michael & Rachel Relf 2017 (updated 2020)

God has established Israel and the IDF (Israel Defence Force) and He has called the young men and women of the Body of Messiah in Israel to serve and to be salt and light during their service.

June

When Israel became a state, there was one known believer in Yeshua (Jesus) in the IDF and today there are over 500. God is raising up a 'Vast Army' of believers in the IDF (Ezekiel 37). With this comes a growing need for spiritual counselling and pastoral support of these young believers who often struggle with many confronting issues such as: life and death, bearing arms, loving our enemies, trauma, isolation, and keeping your faith amidst persecution. The IDF does not provide chaplaincy and instead directs soldiers to seek that from their local faith community.

The Yedidya Centre in Jerusalem serves those who risk their lives for us. We offer them a place of rest from front-line fatigue and a listening heart to share their challenges with the purpose of keeping and strengthening their faith in Yeshua (Jesus). We seek to provide pastoral care, fellowship, counselling and encouragement for soldiers before, during, and after their active duty. The Yedidya Centre also hosts a healing retreat for IDF soldiers as they complete their mandatory service and re-transition into civilian life...

Michael and his wife Rachel are on team at Beit Sar-Shalom Ministries (CPM Israel). Michael has an MA in Biblical Counselling and serves in the reserve IDF. He has been ministering to the believing youth and soldiers for over 18 years in Israel. Michael and Rachel have a son, Gabriel (5 years old) and a daughter, Keren (2 years old). yedidyacentre@gmail.com

Christian Soldiers' Home – Najeeb & Elizabeth Atteih 2019

Pastor Najeeb and Elizabeth Atteih, from the Immanuel Church in Haifa, encourage Arab youth, especially the Christians, to play their part as citizens of Israel and serve in the Israeli Defense Forces (IDF). Najeeb teaches Israeli Arabs about the privileges they enjoy in Israel compared to any other surrounding Arab State! He encourages them to give back to their country and join the army, which many do. Najeeb and Elizabeth are rightly proud of their son, Tino, who has been promoted to the rank of first sergeant and received a special honour. Najeeb and Tino have been among the Arab contingent invited to the Ministry of Defense in Tel Aviv, and have met Prime Minister Netanyahu.

The Immanuel Church has a special ministry to the Arab Christian soldiers. Life can be tough for these young men, as they are not only different in religious background but also differ ethnically and culturally from the majority of their serving colleagues. The Immanuel Church began a Christian Soldiers' Home to support these young Arab soldiers, who have already taken a huge step to enlist. They often suffer persecution from other youth in their home villages because of their army service. This could be manifested by individuals and communities distancing themselves from a soldier or even physical violence. Najeeb has the Father's heart to minister to them and encourage them.

This ministry has even won the approval of the government and Ministry of Defense. Although primarily for Christian soldiers, Muslim and Jewish soldiers are also welcomed. Earlier this year, they had 122 Bedouin, Jewish and Christian Soldiers, with their commanding officers visit their Home and, with true Arab hospitality, they were given a sumptuous breakfast. The soldiers heard and saw the love of God in action. The army, more than most others, understands what Christians are and do! On another occasion, a whole Battalion of 170 Arab soldiers with their commanding officer came to the Soldiers' Home for a celebration. The news has spread to the Givati Brigade (one of Israel's most elite forces), and they are now wanting to visit. These are tremendous opportunities to share the Gospel and the love of the Messiah through Arab believers.

It costs NIS 15,000 (AUD $6,000) per month to keep the Soldiers' Home going. We are now planning the final stage of our upgrade to the Home which involves placing a roof over the whole compound to protect from

June

rain and storm, and give us space to hold small conferences or celebrations. The cost of this operation would be about NIS 167,000 ($70,000). Enquiries and information: immanuel.haifa@gmail.com

Ima's Goodies – Renee Shmuel 2016

'Ima's Goodies' began after a news article portrayed a group of Messianic believers and Christians from Israel in a poor light. I decided to find a way to show the Israeli Defense Force (IDF) that believers of Messiah in Israel and Christians around the world love, pray for and support them. I began to bake treats for the soldiers and share with them the tangible love of Yeshua.

In June 2014, rockets were being fired from Gaza while our soldiers were looking for some teenage boys who had been kidnapped. During our first three months we went out three times a week to the border of Gaza (with borrowed helmets and vests to protect us from rockets and falling shrapnel), visiting between 2,000-3,000 soldiers, taking homemade goodies and cold drinks. We shared the love of Messiah and told them that there are Christians and Messianic Jews supporting them. After this, things started to heat up on the northern borders with Lebanon and Syria. As we travelled north, we came across soldiers, gave them goodies, encouraged, prayed and loved them. We are always welcomed with open arms as some feel they are forgotten. Now, as many as 300 soldiers each week are being encouraged, in addition to other units of Border Patrol Police that we visit regularly in the Judea/Samaria area and the soldiers in our own congregation. We have also been invited to encourage a group of soldiers at the end of every three-month course that they take for leadership skills and commanders the Border Police.

The compulsory military service is usually a very challenging and frightening time for our young men and women. They come up against forces of this world in a physical battle. The knowledge that there are people who pray for safety and wisdom for them while on duty is new to them. The actual cakes or sweets brought to their base are a tangible way to share and say, *Taste and see that the Lord, He is good* (Ps 34:8).

This ministry is breaking up and plowing the hard ground so the seed can fall on good soil. I want these soldiers to look back upon their army service, when they heard about Messiah, Messianic Jews or believers, with a taste in their mouth, literally, wanting more of Yeshua and His goodness.

Renee Shmuel and her husband Gidon, an Israeli Sabra (born in Israel), have been married for over 30 years. They have been part of the Carmel Congregation in Haifa since the beginning. Gidon has been a deacon for over 25 years and Renee serves in the congregation in a variety of ways. They both volunteer with Magen David Adom Ambulance services in Israel. imasgoodies@gmail.com, https://www.imasgoodies.com, https://www.facebook.com/ImasGoodiesIsrael

June Prayer Points - IDF

1. Pray for God's almighty angelic protection over His land. Ps 91
2. Pray for God to expose to Israel every hidden plan of the enemy against her – tunnels, rockets, suicide bombers etc before they can cause harm. Daniel 2:22
3. Pray for the exposing of the corruption in the Palestinian organisations and abuse of funds sent to alleviate the poor that is used to fund tunnel -building and weapons to fight Israel. Lk 8:17
4. Pray for the strangling of funds and blocking of channels that supply the weapons to Hamas and Hezbollah. Pray for countries to stop sending funds when they are used for terrorist purposes. Ps 101:8
5. Pray for the border police and guards to be alert and discerning as to dangers and stop them before they happen. Many more attacks are thwarted than those that actually succeed. Pray for continuous miracles of protection of God's people. Ps 124, Ps 121, Ps 127:1-2

June

6. Pray for physical and mental healing for the people injured in Israel's wars and comfort for grieving families. Pray for those who are living with often life-changing injuries that inhibit them from a normal life. 2 Thess 2:16-17, Hos 6:1
7. Pray for the ministries that assist these people, such as those above, to be able to provide spiritual and material support and lead them to the Lord of all comfort. 2 Cor 1:3-4
8. Pray for those suffering post-traumatic stress as a result of their army service. May God heal their memories, restore their nervous systems and give them a sound mind. 2 Tim1:7 (NKJV)
9. Pray for all the people to find shelter in the four seconds they have after the sirens sound and before the rockets arrive and pray for the children traumatised from the constant fear of dramatic dashes for cover, often in the middle of the night when rockets rain down on them. Lk 18:16, Ps 68:1
10. Pray for all buildings to be equipped with a reinforced bomb shelter. Is 33:15-16
11. Pray for the IDF soldiers to be protected and be accurate when they must fire. Ps 144:1-2
12. The biggest threat to Israel's existence is Iran and its nuclear weapons. Pray for God's timing to be perfect if Israel needs to destroy Iranian nuclear facilities. Jas 1:5-6
13. Pray for the leaders of the IDF and governmental leaders to make wise decisions. Prov 1:7
14. Pray for the iron dome and the new cheaper laser weaponry to be developed quickly and be strengthened and expanded to disperse the rockets before they land. Ps 18:13-14
15. Pray for God's creative answers to overcome incendiary weapons. Is 54:17
16. Pray for the Messianic soldiers and Arab Christians to be good witnesses, find time to be with the Lord and hold fast to the faith in a secular environment. Phil 2:12-16
17. Pray for the believers in the IDF to remain sexually pure during this testing time. Prov chapter 5
18. Pray for life inside the womb to be valued by the mothers and the IDF and the abortion issue align with God's Word. Ps 139:13-16

All Israel Shall be Saved

19. Pray for the gospel to be preached and touch the hearts of those who hate Israel. Matt 5:11-12, 24:14
20. Pray for the children of Palestine to seek truth, despite their minds being poisoned with hatred for their Jewish neighbours. Jn 8:31-32
21. Pray for the Christians living in the Palestinian territories to be bold in their witness and overcome hatred with love. Acts 4:29-31
22. Pray for the salvation of many Palestinians. Pray for dreams and visions of Jesus. Acts 2:17
23. Pray for the Palestinian mothers to protect their children and not allow them to be drawn into performing violent acts that endanger their lives. Prov 22:6
24. Pray for the exposure of the indoctrination of Palestinian children in training and that the international community will not stand for such things as teaching 8-year-old children to shoot at Israeli soldiers. https://www.gatestoneinstitute.org/6259/hamas-camps-child-abuse, https://www1.cbn.com/cbnnews/israel/2020/february/group-launches-campaign-to-lsquo-save-palestinian-child-soldiers-rsquo Lk 17:2
25. Pray for an answer to the Syrian crisis and the blocking of Iranian forces that are becoming entrenched there. Israel helped Syrians who sought needed medical help at the border for many years. Pray they will remember this kindness. Matt 5:16
26. The Golan Heights are critical for Israel's defence as it is a high plateau that overlooks the Sea of Galilee and borders on Syria. Pray that this will stay in Israeli hands. Ps 7:1-2
27. Pray for God to comfort and provide homes and safety for the Syrian refugees who are fleeing the most atrocious situation, traumatised and destitute. Arab pastors, Najeeb and Elizabeth Atteih from Haifa, visit the refugees stuck on the Jordanian border. May God use this lovely couple to help and love them and lead them to Jesus. James 1:27
28. Pray for peace on the Lebanese border. Pray that Lebanon will weed out the Hezbollah militants and restore friendly relations with Israel. Pray that Hezbollah will be exposed as a terrorist organisation. Acts 26:18
29. Thank the Lord for the peace with Jordan and Egypt and pray that they will continue. Pray for Egypt not to allow tunnel-building or supplies for this from their territory. May they build Israel, not destroy it. Is 61:4-5

June

30. Pray for the highway of worship from Egypt to Assyria to be established and praise God that He is a warrior who promises to fight for His people. Is 19:23-25, Zeph 3:17, Zech 14:3.

July
Clearing the Stones

The Fountain of Tears, Arad – a profound, artistic depiction of the suffering of Jesus on the cross and the suffering of the Jewish people during the holocaust.
https://www.fountainoftears.org

Oh, that my head were a spring of water and my eyes a fountain of tears! I would weep day and night for the slain of my people. Jer 9:1 (NIV)

Do not be arrogant toward the branches; but if you are arrogant, remember that it is not you who supports the root, but the root supports you. Rom 11:18

Pass through, pass through the gates! Prepare the way for the people. Build up, build up the highway! Remove the stones. Raise a banner for the nations. Is 62:10 (NIV)

July

When humanity can find no one else to blame for its woes, the Jewish people have always been the scapegoat. Ultimately, it is Satan who stirs the forces to rise up in hatred and anti-Semitism to persecute those who represent God by their very existence. This month we look at this issue, examine an evil root and find God's answer for how to pray for redemption.

9th Av - Turning Mourning into Joy

The book of Zechariah contains some wonderful promises about Israel's restoration. Some of these have been fulfilled in the return from Babylon, but many still lie in the future, waiting to be prayed into being in God's appointed time. Chapter 8 commences:

Then the word of the LORD of hosts came, saying, "Thus says the LORD of hosts, 'I am exceedingly jealous for Zion, yes, with great wrath I am jealous for her.' Thus says the LORD, 'I will return to Zion and will dwell in the midst of Jerusalem. Then Jerusalem will be called the City of Truth, and the mountain of the LORD of hosts will be called the Holy Mountain.'" Zech 8:1-3

It continues with promises to bring the people back so the streets are filled with people, make Israel His people again, rebuild the temple, prosper the land and make them a blessing. It then mentions four fasts that will be redeemed:

Then the word of the LORD of hosts came to me, saying, "Thus says the LORD of hosts, 'The fast of the fourth, the fast of the fifth, the fast of the seventh and the fast of the tenth months will become joy, gladness, and cheerful feasts for the house of Judah; so love truth and peace.'" Zech 8:18-19

These fasts all have to do with the fall of the city of Jerusalem leading up to the capture and exile of the people to Babylon. Taken chronologically, these were:

In the 9th year of the Judean King Zedekiah's reign, in the 10th month on the 10th day, Nebuchadnezzar and his armies arrived in Jerusalem and began to build a siege wall against the city (Jer 39:1, 52:4). This lasted for 18 months.

In the 11th year, the 4th month and 9th day, the wall was breached and the people fled at night. The famine forced by the siege meant there was no food left in the city (Jer 39:2; 52:6). Zedekiah was captured and taken away to Babylon.

In the fifth month, called Av, on the 9th-10th day (586 BCE), Nebuzaradan, the captain of Nebuchadnezzar's guard, came to Jerusalem and burnt the Temple, the king's palace and the houses and flattened the walls, taking many captive to Babylon (Jer 52:12-16).

In his place, Gedaliah was made governor (2 Kgs 25:22-26) as a Babylonian subject. However, Ishmael, a descendent of the royal family, gathered a small group of men and killed Gedaliah in the 7th month (Jer 41:1-2).

Of these four fast days, only the 9th Av is a major commemoration in the Jewish calendar today and is remembered as a day of fasting and mourning. The importance of this day is that the second Temple was also destroyed on the same day in the Hebrew calendar and numerous other tragedies have also occurred since then on the same day. It occurs in July-August. If it falls on a Sabbath, the fast is held the following day. The dates for the upcoming years are: 2020, July 29-30; 2021, July 17-18; 2022, Aug 6-7; 2023, July 26-27 2024, Aug 12-13; 2025, Aug 2-3

Major Events that Happened on 9th Av

- The spies' good report of the land was rejected by the Hebrew people (Num 13:1-14:24)

July

- 586 BCE Destruction of the first Temple by the Babylonians
- 70 CE Destruction of the second Temple by the Romans
- 135 CE Final defeat of the 2nd Jewish Revolt at Betar, 100,000 slaughtered
- 136 CE Jerusalem was rebuilt as a Roman city, Aelia Capitolina, and the land was renamed Palaestina to destroy the Hebrew connection
- 1096 CE Pope Urban II declared the first crusade. Tens of thousands of Jews were killed by the Crusaders. In Jerusalem they herded them into the synagogue and burnt them to death.
- 1290 CE Jews were expelled from England. Many drowned trying to reach Europe. Jews could not return to Britain until 1655.
- 1492 CE Spanish inquisition. 200,000 Jews were expelled from Spain. Those who could not escape were told 'convert or be killed'.
- 1555 CE Papal Bull of Pope Paul IV. 3,000 Jews were put into a ghetto in Rome and forced to wear a yellow patch.
- 1914 CE Germany declared war on Russia
- 1941 CE Himmler received approval from the Nazi Party for the 'Final Solution'
- 1942 CE Treblinka extermination camp in Poland was opened. 800,000+ Jews were transported from the Warsaw Ghetto and murdered.

Christian Moves to Right Many Wrongs

In 2018, two Christians from the Jewish-Christian organisation 'Root Source' took the initiative to turn this day of Jewish mourning into joy and gladness as Zechariah 8:19 prophesies.

Few Christians know the shocking history of Christian persecution of Jews but Jews know it well, so Root Source directors Bob O'Dell and Ray Montgomery compiled a list of over 500 specific massed incidents of Christian persecution of Jews throughout history, including pogroms, lynchings, riots, forcing Jews to wear special clothing, expelling Jews, anti-Semitic writings from Church leaders, setting fire to synagogues with Jews trapped inside, forced conversions, falsely accusing Jews of killing Christian children to use their blood to make matzah and the rape and murder of Jews.

All Israel Shall be Saved

You can download a full list (all 43 pages) of the atrocities committed against the Jewish people by the church at the following website. It is sobering reading. https://root-source.com/wp-content/uploads/2018/07/LIST-of-Persecution-of-Jews-by-Christians-V1.02-Aug-2.pdf

Is it any wonder that Jewish people find it hard to accept our loving Saviour when such atrocities over so many thousands of years have been done to them in His name? On many occasions, people went from a church service (often Christmas or Easter) immediately out to slaughter Jews (and also Muslims) believing the lie that the Jews killed Jesus (*He gave His life* - Matt 20:28) or the total fabrication that Jews mixed the blood in their sacrifices.

Replacement Theology

How did these atrocities come about in the name of Jesus? The answer is found in two words - Replacement Theology. This is a false interpretation of the Bible that still persists to this day. It fails to accept that when God makes an eternal covenant, He will keep His covenant.

Holocaust memorial Jerusalem

The word of the LORD came to Jeremiah, saying, "Thus says the LORD, 'If you can break My covenant for the day and My covenant for the night, so that day and night will not be at their appointed time, then My covenant may also be broken with David My servant so that he will not have a son to reign on his throne, and with the Levitical priests, My ministers. As the host of heaven cannot be counted and the sand of the sea cannot be measured, so I will multiply the descendants of David My servant and the Levites who minister to Me.'" Jer 33:19-22

The argument for Replacement Theology says that, because most of Israel rejected the

July

Messiah at His first coming, God has cast them off and replaced them with the church as His new Israel in the world. This denies that fact that God wants His entity to be 'one new man in Christ' comprised of both Jews and Gentiles (Eph 2:15). Replacement theology interprets all New Testament Scriptures that mention Israel to mean the church, with Israel now cursed of God. It misses that Christians were called to be heirs together *with* Israel, and *not instead of* Israel. This thinking meant Jews were told to convert or leave and in many cases were killed. They were no longer allowed to live as the Bible instructed them and even Jewish converts had to deny their God-given national identity and heritage to embrace a 'Christian' one that by this time was based on pagan festivals.

Paul warned us against such arrogance in Rom 11:18-21. because if God can cast off Israel, then what about us? Have we really been so obedient? Are we not unfaithful like they were? Thank God for His grace. Covenant is the basis for our hope and covenant is the basis for the Jewish hope as well. If God can break His covenant to either people group then we have no assurance of salvation. But God is faithful and will not break His promises but will bring His Word to pass and fulfil all that He has promised – to Jew and Gentile.

It is a trustworthy statement: For if we died with Him, we will also live with Him; If we endure, we will also reign with Him; If we deny Him, He also will deny us; If we are faithless, He remains faithful, for He cannot deny Himself. 2 Tim 2:11-13

Replacement theology ignores several clear Scriptures that say that the rejection of the Jews of their Messiah is related to several 'until' clauses:

- Romans 11:25 – until the fullness of the Gentiles has come in

Paul teaches us that Israel's rejection was partial and for a limited time and purpose: their rejection was for our sake.

All Israel Shall be Saved

For I do not want you, brethren, to be uninformed of this mystery—so that you will not be wise in your own estimation—that a partial hardening has happened to Israel until the fullness of the Gentiles has come in. Rom 11:25

But by their transgression salvation has come to the Gentiles, to make them jealous. Now if their transgression is riches for the world and their failure is riches for the Gentiles, how much more will their fulfillment be!... For if their rejection is the reconciliation of the world, what will their acceptance be but life from the dead? Rom 11:11-12, 15

- Luke 21:24 – until the times of the Gentiles are fulfilled

and they will fall by the edge of the sword, and will be led captive into all the nations; and Jerusalem will be trampled underfoot by the Gentiles until the times of the Gentiles are fulfilled.

- Matt 23:39, Lk 13:35 – until you say 'Baruch Haba b'Shem Adonai' (i.e. welcome)

For I say to you, from now on you will not see Me until you say, 'Blessed is He who comes in the name of the Lord!'"

- Hosea 5:15 - until Israel repents

I will go away and return to My place until they acknowledge their guilt and seek My face; In their affliction they will earnestly seek Me.

Replacement Theology in History

Replacement theology has been around a long time. Many of our most esteemed early Christian Fathers perpetrated this teaching. Justin Martyr, who wrote around 160 CE was possibly the first major proponent of Replacement Theology. Irenaeus, Tertullian, Origen and Eusebius followed and in 325 CE at the Council of Nicaea, the church was officially severed from its Jewish roots. At that time, Easter was moved to coincide with the

July

Babylonian festival of Ishtar (Easter) and Christians were forbidden to participate in biblical feasts including Passover.

John Chrysostom, St Augustine and St Jerome (Latin Vulgate Bible translator) followed in the same vein of Jew-hatred, blaming them for killing Jesus. Oppression, subjugation, murders and expulsions from country to country followed for the next several hundred years at the hands of the church, such that the Jews preferred to be under Islamic subjugation rather than Christian domination. The Crusades, in Jesus' name, wiped out the Jewish population of almost every city they came through.

It was not just the Catholic Church that persecuted Jews. Many will be shocked to learn that near the end of his life, Martin Luther wrote one of the most venomous books ever written against the Jews, called '*On the Jews and their Lies*'.
https://www.jewishvirtuallibrary.org/martin-luther-quot-the-jews-and-their-lies-quote.

Luther's Teaching – *On the Jews and their Lies* **excerpt 1543**

> What shall we Christians do with this rejected and condemned people, the Jews?... I shall give you my sincere advice:

Martin Luther

> First, to set fire to their synagogues or schools and to bury and cover with dirt whatever will not burn, so that no man will ever again see a stone or cinder of them. This is to be done in honor of our Lord and of Christendom, so that God might see that we are Christians, and do not condone or knowingly tolerate such public lying, cursing, and blaspheming of his Son and of his Christians...
>
> Second, I advise that their houses also be razed and destroyed...

Third, I advise that all their prayer books and Talmudic writings, in which such idolatry, lies, cursing and blasphemy are taught, be taken from them...

Fourth, I advise that their rabbis be forbidden to teach henceforth on pain of loss of life and limb. For they have justly forfeited the right to such an office by holding the poor Jews captive with the saying of Moses (Deuteronomy 17 [:10 ff.]) in which he commands them to obey their teachers on penalty of death, although Moses clearly adds: "what they teach you in accord with the law of the Lord." Those villains ignore that...

Fifth, I advise that safe conduct on the highways be abolished completely for the Jews. For they have no business in the countryside, since they are not lords, officials, tradesmen, or the like. Let they stay at home...

Sixth, I advise that usury be prohibited to them and that all cash and treasure of silver and gold be taken from them and put aside for safekeeping. The reason for such a measure is that, as said above, they have no other means of earning a livelihood than usury, and by it they have stolen and robbed from us all they possess...

Seventh, I commend putting a flail, an ax, a hoe, a spade, a distaff, or a spindle into the hands of young, strong Jews and Jewesses and letting them earn their bread in the sweat of their brow, as was imposed on the children of Adam (Gen 3[:19])...

My essay, I hope, will furnish a Christian (who in any case has no desire to become a Jew) with enough material not only to defend himself against the blind, venomous Jews, but also to become the foe of the Jews' malice, lying, and cursing, and to understand not only that their belief is false but that they are surely possessed by all devils. May Christ, our dear Lord, convert them mercifully and preserve us steadfastly and immovably in the knowledge of him, which is eternal life. Amen.

Hitler later quoted Luther's views to justify the Holocaust and the murder of 6 million Jews. Germany was supposedly a Christian nation because of its roots back to Luther, and therefore Jewish people see the Holocaust as an outworking of the Christian religion. God forbid!

Redeeming the 9th of Av - The Healing Begins

The passage in Zechariah chapter 8 where the fast days are mentioned, including the 9th Av, prophesies a turning of the sadness into joy. These fasts:

...will become joy, gladness, and cheerful feasts for the house of Judah; so love truth and peace.' (v 19)

How will this happen? The passage continues:

Holocaust memorial Thessalonika

Thus says the LORD of hosts, 'It will yet be that peoples will come, even the inhabitants of many cities. The inhabitants of one will go to another, saying, "Let us go at once to entreat the favor of the LORD, and to seek the LORD of hosts; I will also go." So many peoples and mighty nations will come to seek the LORD of hosts in Jerusalem and to entreat the favor of the LORD.' Thus says the LORD of hosts, 'In those days ten men from all the nations will grasp the garment of a Jew, saying, "Let us go with you, for we have heard that God is with you."' Zech 8:20-23

Nations and the 9th Av

Root Source has begun an initiative to heal the wounds following the strategy mentioned in Zechariah. Part of the action involves coming to Israel to repent and stand with the Jewish people. They will hold an annual event that is based in repentance for the hurt that we as Christians have caused the Jewish people. Those in the nations can read the book of Lamentations (as do the Jews), repent before the Lord and make the list known to other Christians. They also encourage Christians to sign a declaration acknowledging, "We the undersigned recognise the long and horrific history of anti-Semitic atrocities committed against Jews in the name of Christ. We repent for these actions, pray to God to continue turning the hearts of Christians to a true love for His Chosen People, and submit this declaration to the representatives of Israel and the Jewish People". You can sign the declaration and find more resources at https://9-av.com.

July Prayer - Repentance for Atrocities and Replacement Theology

1. Let us own this dreadful history and repent before the throne of God for these atrocities done in Jesus' name. Daniel also repented on behalf of his people. Dan 9:3-5, 8-10
2. If Jewish people mention this history to you, don't argue, but say you are so sorry that people have so abused Jesus' name and apologise on their behalf for the hurt caused to them and their people. A humble heart breaks many arguments. 1 Jn 1:10
3. Search the Scriptures for the truth. Thank Jesus for choosing to give His life. Mk 10:45
4. Jesus never blamed His accusers but asked the Father to forgive them for they did not know what they were doing. Ask the Lord for this same understanding and heart. Lk 23:34
5. Ask the Lord to change the hard heart of the church towards His chosen people. Mk 12:30-31
6. Pray for more Christians to have the revelation of God's plans for the Jews and the Gentiles as outlined in Romans chapter 11.
7. Repent for the church falling into the pride of replacement theology. Is 13:11
8. Pray for the Jews to be able to forgive those who have hurt them so they can be healed. Matt 6:12
9. Thank God that He has promised to wipe away their sin and give them a new heart. Zech 13:1, Ezek 11:19

July

10. Pray for the church to see the Jews as our brothers and sisters as God's children. Gal 3:7-8
11. Pray for the 'one new man' of Jews and Gentiles to emerge more fully. Eph 2:14-16
12. Pray for the Jews to know that believers are now God's temple indwelt with the Holy Spirit of God, and not to pine for the last one. 1 Pet 2:4-5
13. Thank God that He has not rejected His covenant people. Rom 11:1
14. Pray for Israeli Jewish and Arab believers to unite in the love of Jesus. 2 Cor 13:11
15. Pray for anti-Semitism to be exposed and condemned. Ps 69:4
16. Pray for God to protect His people from attacks. Ps 31:20
17. Pray for God to draw the Jews to come home to Israel. At least they now have an option, whereas in previous generations they were simply annihilated. Hos 11:3-4
18. Thank God that the Jews have given us the Messiah. Rom 11:11
19. Pray for more pastors to see that Jesus is Jewish and delve into the Jewish roots of Christianity rather that worshiping a false Gentile God. Matt 1:1
20. Pray for the church to be grafted in again to the true Jewish Jesus. Rom 11:17-18
21. Pray for more Christians to come alongside the Jewish people on 9th Av so that the pain may be turned to joy. Zech 8:19
22. Pray for the Holocaust to be taught in Western schools as many young people now do not understand what happened. May this knowledge prevent a repeat of the evil. Jer 6:15-17
23. Pray that the Protestant churches based on Luther will be discerning and openly begin to repent for the false parts of his teachings and not be led astray. 1 Jn 4:1
24. Pray for the Roman Catholic Church also to repent for cutting Christianity off from its Jewish roots at the Council of Nicaea in 325 CE. 2 Cor 11:13-15
25. Pray that the BDS (Boycott, Divestment and Sanctions) movement, that aims to cripple Israel economically, will fail and be condemned and outlawed worldwide as it is only a mask for anti-Semitism. Ps 5:4-7
26. Pray for many nations to come up to Jerusalem to pray before the Lord. Zech 8:22

All Israel Shall be Saved

27. Pray for those ten from every language to come and recognise what God is doing and grasp the prayer tassels of a godly Jewish man. Zech 8:23
28. Pray for Israel to recognise that God is with them and not put their trust in man. Zech 8:23
29. Pray for the Muslim nations to realise that God is with the Jews and come alongside Israel that they may receive the blessing. Gen 12:3, Zech 8:13
30. Pray that Jerusalem may truly become the City of Truth. Zech 8:3
31. Pray into fulfilment, 'They shall be My people and I will be their God in truth and righteousness'. Zech 8:8

August
Removing the Veil

But to this day whenever Moses is read, a veil lies over their heart; but whenever a person turns to the Lord, the veil is taken away. 2 Cor 3:15-16

For the weapons of our warfare are not of the flesh, but divinely powerful for the destruction of fortresses. We are destroying...every lofty thing raised up against the knowledge of God, and we are taking every thought captive to the obedience of Christ. 2 Cor 10:4-5

So if all the world is being greatly enriched through their failure, and through their fall great spiritual wealth is given to the non-Jewish people, imagine how much more will Israel's awakening bring to us all! Romans 11:12 (The Passion Translation)

August

This month we will look at the different Jewish groups, and focus our prayers on the ultra-orthodox. The ultra-orthodox are by far the most difficult Jewish group to reach with the gospel. They are steeped in tradition and staunchly resist any threats to their protected beliefs and lifestyle. They are the modern-day Pharisees still opposed to the gospel.

The Pharisees

Last month we looked at persecution of Jews from outside but there is also a persecution of Jews by other Jews occurring today. This is happening from some sectors of the ultra-orthodox community against the Messianic believers and can be very violent. It is well planned and well coordinated, chiefly by an 'anti-missionary' group called 'Yad L'achim', although another group, LeHava, has more recently caused trouble also. Their strategy begins with heckling and stone-throwing around meeting times and posting pictures of believers on lampposts telling Jews to avoid these 'dangerous missionaries'. It continues with trying to get councils and landowners to cancel contracts for renting buildings. The next steps are things such as slashing tyres and breaking windscreens of believers' cars or throwing rocks through  windows of houses or ministry buildings where they meet. Some have set buildings alight, planted bombs, tried to close down believers' businesses (sometimes successfully) and cursed the believers.

Just as the Pharisees held the power and controlled the spiritual atmosphere in Jesus' day, so the Hassidim have a powerful influence in modern-day Israeli politics. In the government, the ultra-orthodox Shas party demands control of immigration and education. They therefore block Jewish believers from making aliya, sometimes refuse visa and passport renewals from believers and long-term Christian residents, and of late are even blocking believers from gaining marriage certificates in Israel. Especially when congregations have baptisms for Jewish believers, they will turn up in their hundreds to protest loudly in the streets and disturb the meetings, even using violence causing destruction and injury, as happened in Be'er Sheva in 2005. When complaints are made to the police, they generally do little and when court cases arise, they rarely get a fair hearing. Thank God for the Jerusalem Institute of Justice, founded in 2004 by Calev Myers (JPF 2009), that is legally supporting individual believers and congregations in these types of lawsuits. This is not to suggest that these actions or tactics are used by all ultra-orthodox Jews, since many orthodox Jews support the believers, but it is a fringe minority that are loud and aggressive.

Jewish Denominations – Rabbi Harold Vallins 2004

Judaism is as much splintered into different groups as is Christianity. Many people regard Judaism as a homogenous group but in some respects, their beliefs and doctrines almost make them different religions. Unlike Christianity, Judaism is not held together by a creed, but rather a way of life with a call to holiness, the outworking of which takes a variety of forms. In fact, most Jews are secular and their knowledge of Judaism is very basic and more reliant upon tradition than Biblical understanding. Festivals such Passover and Purim, and rites of passage like the Bar/Bat Mitzvah, have assured the continuation of a minimal knowledge of the Biblical stories, but few Jews in this category have anything other than a child-like understanding of God. Here is a very brief summary of the main groups within Judaism.

Ultra-Orthodox

Into this category we would put such groups as Chabad, Hassidim, Lubavitch and Haredim. They all believe that the Torah (the Five Books of Moses) is the absolute word of God. Their two main basic books are the Bible and the Talmud, though they also draw heavily on Kabbalistic teachings. Their basic belief is that God is One and only One, in direct opposition to the teaching of the Trinity. In practice, they will adhere strictly to the laws concerning the Sabbath, the dietary laws, the study of the Talmud and will wear the distinctive black clothes worn by their founder, the Baal Shem Tov (Rabbi Israel ben Eliezer, 1700-1760). They will live within walking distance to their place of worship, thus establishing very close-knit communities or 'ghettos'.

Orthodox or Modern Orthodox

Most of these Jews will acknowledge the authority of the Torah and the Talmud but will know very little of the Torah and even less of the Talmud. Their basic teaching is God is One – indivisible, uniquely One. Israel is central to their identity as Jews and they regard 'aliya' (immigration to Israel) as very important. They will maintain a culturally identifiable Jewish way of life - attend Synagogue services on the main Jewish festivals, observe the dietary laws (at least within the home) and will ensure that their children receive a Jewish education usually at a Jewish day school. Although their services are mainly in Hebrew, very few will be able to read it or understand what they read.

Reform Judaism, also known as Liberal Judaism

This movement originated in the 18th century in Germany and grew widely in the 19th century. It began when Moses Mendelssohn translated and published the Torah into German. This was the first time that lay people were able to know what the Torah contained and many were dismayed and rejected much of what they could now read and understand. In particular, this gave rise to the teaching that the Torah was not the literal word of God but was inspired by God and written over many centuries by different groups of men. They accepted the moral and ethical codes of the Torah and a belief in a monotheistic God. However, there was no longer an expectation of a physical Messiah or literal resurrection from the dead. There was a very strong desire to 'move' Judaism into the modern times. The laws of the Sabbath were greatly relaxed, the vernacular was introduced into the services, men and women were allowed to sit together and the dietary laws became optional. Their services are shorter than those of the Orthodox and about 60% is in English. The Reform movement mushroomed as a result of the great migration of Continental European Jews to England and America in the 20th century and is now the largest group within Judaism.

Conservative Judaism

This developed as a backlash to what some of the more traditionally minded Reform Jews regarded as "throwing the baby out with the bath water". They hold a much more traditional view of the literal nature of the Torah. They accept the moral teachings of the Torah as binding but interpret the traditions in the light of modern times. They also acknowledge the Talmud and other oral traditions as authoritative guides to their Jewish way of life. The central focus of Conservatism is the idea of Jewish peoplehood rather than a belief system. They reintroduced a greater amount of Hebrew into their services, strongly recommended the observance of the dietary laws and made strong recommendations for a more traditional observance of the Sabbath laws.

Messianic Judaism

This is still in its infancy at the moment. The movement has re-emerged in America and is gaining a hold in the main Jewish centers such as New York State, Philadelphia, California and Florida. The movement recognises Jesus as the Jewish Messiah, accepts the validity of the New Testament and teaches about the Trinity. The main body of Messianic Jews is led by the International Alliance of Messianic Hebrew Congregations. The last known accepted number of Messianic Jews was 2% of world Jewry.

Rabbi Harold Vallins was ordained a rabbi in 1970 at the Leo Baeck Theological College (Reform Judaism) in London. He found Yeshua in 1998 (see the Testimonies section in the appendix). As a result of embracing Yeshua as his personal Messiah, he lost his congregation and his family. He was a former rabbi at Beit HaMashiach Messianic Congregation in Melbourne, associated with 'Celebrate Messiah'. He passed away in 2009.

August

The Ultra-Orthodox in Israel

The ultra-orthodox are the strictest sector of the Jews and zealously practise Rabbinic Judaism as did their spiritual forefathers, the biblical Pharisees to which Paul belonged (Acts 26:4,5). Their black coats and hats, beards, tzitzit (tassels) and side curls make them the most easily recognised group amongst the orthodox Jewish men. Women wear long skirts, long blouses and a head covering, and spend most of their time caring for their large families (average of six children). In Jerusalem, the majority of the ultra-orthodox live in the suburb of Mea Shearim, and belong to the Hassidic group ('the pious ones').

The Hassidim believe that, in addition to the written law of Moses, there was an oral law, without which one cannot understand the hidden, deeper meaning of the written law. The men spend all day studying the Bible and the Talmud in a yeshiva (religious school). The Talmud is a collection of Jewish law and tradition which was collated from the teachings of the elders around 400 CE (Palestinian Talmud) or approximately 500 CE (Babylonian Talmud). It consists of the Mishnah (commentaries - similar to board meeting minutes of rabbis discussing a Bible passage) and the Gemara (rabbinic analysis and commentary on the Mishnah). They are heavily influenced by the kabbalistic writings (see below).

The men usually do not work regular jobs so the community is poor. They receive welfare payments from the government and funding from Jews in the diaspora. They live in closed, close-knit communities and shun the outside world, rarely venturing beyond their ghettos. The leaders (the rabbis or 'tsaddik' – holy ones) wield much power and hold total control over the lives of the younger members and keep them dependent on the rabbinic system, financially, emotionally and spiritually. In the synagogues and

All Israel Shall be Saved

yeshivas, a student may not read the Scriptures alone - he must ask the Rabbi or look at a commentary. Despite their full-time study, most Torah students have little grasp of the Bible and rarely have any personal relationship with God. *They have a zeal for God but not in accordance with knowledge* (Rom 10:2). Saul was one of these but God appeared to him in a light and voice from heaven, transforming his life (Acts chapter 9).

If they become believers, they have no skills to obtain jobs, no source of income, will be cut off from their families and friends and be persecuted by their community. One man who came to faith was blindfolded by the religious police, kidnapped and asked to renounce his faith. When he refused, he was beaten, stripped, had urine thrown at him, his face rubbed in dog excreta, his family threatened and told he would never see his children again. He was then subjected to daily public humiliation in the yeshiva and finally ex-communicated when the entire community took a vow of silence. Believers need massive support to survive against such odds.

The 'religious police' are usually the 'Yad L'Achim' (A Hand to Brethren) group. Its main focus is to counter 'missionary' activity, with the aim of rescuing and re-converting Jews to Judaism. Their main targets are Messianic Jews and Jehovah's Witnesses. They send out under-cover spies to expose converts then set about 'biblically' de-programming those who have 'been deceived'. Many Messianic families and groups have suffered terrible harassment and hurt from them.

Ultra-orthodox Jews are the most unreached people group in the world. This group, numbering one million in Israel, 300,000 in New York, and possibly 5,000 in Australia, need particular prayer, as Jesus said in Matthew 23:39 that He would return when the Scribes and the Pharisees said, 'Baruch haba b'Shem Adonai' – meaning these are the ones who must welcome the Messiah.

August

Kabbalah

Kabbalah is the esoteric mystical teaching of Judaism and has to do with gaining 'hidden knowledge' to understand the 'concealed' meaning of the Torah. This knowledge is supposedly hidden in the words, letters and numerical values of the letters of the Hebrew text (called Gematria). The knowledge is expressed in symbols and metaphor, so the literal meaning of the text is virtually lost. For the kabbalists, God (referred to as Ein Sof – meaning 'without end') is transcendent and holy and cannot interact directly with His creation. Like freemasonry, which derives much from kabbalah, one must then embark on an 'ascent of the soul' to reach Him, the steps of which are often depicted as the kabbalistic 'Tree of Life'. However, it resembles more the knowledge gained from the tree of the knowledge of good and evil containing many teachings and practices that are in direct opposition to the Scriptures, such as re-incarnation (Heb 9:27) and 'evil inclination' rather than sin, with no concept of grace. Kabbalists engage in occultism, speaking curses and seeking spirits from another world (Deut 18:10-11, Matt 12:33). The scarlet threads the orthodox in Jerusalem try to sell you are associated with this, as are magic charms such as the hamsa (the hand with an eye to ward off evil) depicted on much jewellery and many Jewish souvenirs.

The origins of Kabbalah are shrouded in mystery, but some attribute the Zohar (one of their chief books) to the 2nd century Rabbi Shimon bar Yohai who claimed to have had visitations from Moses and Elijah who revealed the secrets of Zohar to him. Invoking the dead is forbidden in Scripture (Deut 18:10-12). The city of Safed, near where Rabbi bar Yohai died, is still the spiritual centre and stronghold of Kabbalah. Tens of thousands (particularly the Hassidim) make pilgrimage to Safed each year, to pray at the graves of dead rabbis, especially at the festival of Lag B'Omer. Safed is the 'city set on a hill' that Jesus referred to in His Sermon on the Mount (Matt 5:14), as it can be seen from the Mount of Beatitudes. Pray that it will be restored to its destiny – to be a source of light in the darkness.

Paul tells us that the mysteries of God are now revealed and are to be found in Christ (Col 2:2-3). True wisdom leads us to the knowledge and character of Jesus, and must be consistent with the Word of God (1 Cor 1:18-24). God has descended to earth (Jn 1:14), revealed Himself in the visible human form of Jesus (Col 2:9-10) and any man-made efforts to ascend to God by our own efforts or through hidden knowledge will lead us into the clutch of the enemy (Col 2:8).

Judea and Samaria

There are many ultra-orthodox living in well over 100 settlements in the biblical heartland of Judea and Samaria, which largely corresponds to the area conquered by Joshua, including most of the cities we know from the Bible. The pioneers who live there today do so because they believe the Bible and have returned to the land with faith that God will give it to them. They are putting their feet on the land, not just their words into the air. This is a laudable spirit. If President Trump's Peace Plan can be implemented, many of these settlements will be annexed to Israel. However, there are very few believers in Yeshua amongst them. Pray for God to send sensitive Holy Spirit-filled evangelists and raise up at least a small group of believers to witness His love in the midst of every settlement.

August Prayer Points – The Ultra-Orthodox

I'm sure the apostle Paul is still interceding in Heaven for his compatriots. If God can change Saul into Paul with a mighty vision from heaven, He can deal with those with the same spirit today.

1. Pray for the closed ultra-orthodox society to be broken open so the light of God can come in. Is 9:2
2. Pray for dreams and visions for those caught in ultra-orthodoxy. Most of those who have come to believe have had supernatural visitations from God. Joel 2:28-29, Acts 9:3-5
3. Pray for the fire of God to fall on the yeshivas where they study and for the Spirit of God to come upon the students and give them a new heart. Acts 2:1-4, Ezek 36:25-27

August

4. Pray for the occult spirit of kabbalah to be smashed. Much of this is satanic although one of their writings does actually say that Jesus was the Messiah! 2 Cor 10:3-6
5. Pray for false leaders to be removed and true shepherds to be raised up. Ezek chapter 34
6. Pray for the satanic strongholds to be broken. Their writings revealed through the appearance of dead prophets and held 'secret' for millennia are not from God. Pray for them to seek the Holy Spirit, not the spirits of dead rabbis. 1 Cor 2:1-13
7. Pray for the Scriptures to come alive by the revelation of the Holy Spirit for the yeshiva students. 2 Tim 2:25-26
8. Pray for the Hassidim to read and understand the literal biblical text. Ps 119:65-72
9. Pray for them to seek truth and not tradition and to focus on the Scriptures and not on the teachings of the rabbis. Jn 8:32, Heb 4:12
10. Pray for the spirit of religion to be broken off them and the scales to fall from their eyes. 2 Cor 3:14-18
11. Pray for them to seek true relationship with God as Moses and David had, and not be satisfied with dead words. Ex 33:11, 17-19
12. Pray for more workers to be willing to pay the price and go and minister to the ultra-orthodox. Matt 9:37-38
13. Pray for New Testaments to be got into the community and not be burnt before they are read. Ps 119:43-44
14. Pray for the organisation 'Yad L'achim' and other groups which exist to persecute the Messianic Jews. Pray for the Lord to bring conviction of sin upon them. Jn 16:7-11
15. Pray for a revelation of Messiah to the persecutors. Pray for God to reveal Himself as the resurrected Lord. Jn 20:26-28
16. It was the religious leadership that rejected Jesus, not the average person, so this group needs to repent and welcome Him back. Matt 23:39
17. Pray for the orthodox to recognise the Messiah as they utter the Messianic greeting at Sukkot (Ps 118:19-26). Praise God that some ultra-orthodox are beginning to find the Lord and come out from their closed communities. They are the modern first fruit of the harvest. James 1:18

All Israel Shall be Saved

18. Pray for those Christian-Messianic organisations working amongst this group. They usually have to remain hidden as they will be targeted and highly persecuted. Ruth 2:12
19. Believers are usually pursued by those who would seek to enslave them again. Pray that the safe houses for those who have converted will be kept hidden. Ps 91
20. Pray for the believers to be given a great measure of love to love their persecutors. Matt 5:43-45
21. Pray that there will be enough safe houses and support for the new believers. 1 Sam 22:23
22. Pray for the new believers to be able to withstand the family pressures of being disowned by their family and community for accepting Yeshua. Matt 19:29
23. Pray for the believers to be able to persevere and hold strong to the Lord against peer pressure and cling to God through all opposition which would seek to drag them back again. 1 Pet 1:3-9
24. Pray for strength for many who are mentally tortured and even physically tortured to try to get them to deny Jesus. 2 Tim 2:10-13
25. When the ultra-orthodox come to Jesus, they have no means of support as they do not have professional or vocational skills to earn a living. Pray for training places and jobs for converts. Ps 18:33-36
26. Pray for their discipleship as they grow to know the Lord and walk with Him on a daily basis. Gal chapter 5
27. Pray for them to be Spirit-filled and learn to hear the voice of the Spirit guiding them. Jn 14:26-27
28. Pray for their physical provision, as they come out of the society with nothing but the clothes they stand in. Lk 12:24
29. Pray for their emotional healing from woundedness. Is 40:1-2
30. Pray for a spirit of discernment between the true and the false of what they have been taught in the past. Phil 1:9-11
31. Pray for total deliverance from the demonic spirits to be broken over them so they are truly a 'new creation in Christ'. 2 Cor 5:17

September

Opening a Cleansing Fountain

Sukkot at the Western Wall - men with Lulavs

Behold, I tell you a mystery; we shall not all sleep, but we will all be changed, in a moment, in the twinkling of an eye, at the last trumpet; for the trumpet will sound, and the dead will be raised imperishable, and we will be changed. 1 Cor 15:51-52

In that day a fountain will be opened for the house of David and for the inhabitants of Jerusalem, for sin and for impurity. Zech 13:1

Now on the last day, the great day of the feast [of Tabernacles], Jesus stood and cried out saying, "If anyone is thirsty, let him come to Me and drink. He who believes in Me, as the Scripture said, 'From his innermost being will flow rivers of living water'". John 7:37-38

September

The Autumn Festivals normally begin in September, although they can commence as late as early October. Like the Spring Festivals, which prophetically told of the slain lamb, the sinless offering, the first fruit resurrection from the dead and the beginning of the new covenant era, so the latter feasts prophetically speak of the end of the current era. Yeshua fulfilled the early feasts with His first coming as Saviour and Redeemer. He will fulfil the Fall festivals at His second coming as King.

The Feast of Trumpets – Yom HaTruah or Rosh HaShanah Lev 23:24, Num 29:1

This festival is commemorated on the first day of the seventh month, called Tishrei. The Hebrew word 'truah' is the name of one of the blasts made on the trumpet which was used as an alarm. The root of the word is 'rua' which means a victory shout over the enemy (Josh 6:20, Zeph 3:14-17). It was heard when the ark was brought into Jerusalem (I Sam 4:5) and at the dedication of the Temple (Ezra 3:11). The shofar/trumpet (ram or deer's horn or two silver trumpets) is blown in the synagogues 100 times at the Feast of Trumpets – 30 times at 3 different points in the liturgy and 10 at the end. It is meant to be an wake-up call (Amos 3:6, Zeph 1:14,16) and cause one to tremble and reflect before one's Maker. It ushers in 10 Days of Awe before the Day of Atonement, during which the people prepare to face the Judge of the Earth and to get their hearts and affairs in order before God and their fellow man.

Birobidzan Synagogue. Photo Lawrence Hirsch

The more common name for this festival is Rosh HaShanah which means

All Israel Shall be Saved

'head of the year'. It is celebrated as the Jewish civil New Year, although the biblical year begins in Nisan, in March-April. In Jewish tradition, the books of Heaven are opened on the Feast of Trumpets and closed on Yom Kippur, at which time one's fate is sealed. Only during these 10 days can the verdict be altered (Dan 7:10, Mal 3:16-18, Rev 20:11-15, 21:27).

The trumpet was sounded on the mountain at Mt Sinai (Ex 19:16-20). In the desert, trumpets were used to gather the people, to give marching orders, to remind God before going to war and to announce sacred assemblies (Num 10:1-10, Ps 81:3). They were sounded later to muster the army or sound an alarm (Jud 3:27, 7:22, Neh 4:20, Ezek 33:3,6). At the sound of the trumpets the walls of Jericho fell (Josh 6:4-5,16,20) and they were blown at the coronation of the king (1 Kgs 1:34, 2 Kgs 11:14). Every Sabbath year the priests were commanded to read the Torah publicly to teach the Word of God (Deut 31:9-13), which Ezra did on the first day of the seventh month (this month) from morning till midday (Neh chapter 8).

Most important of all is that Jesus associated the trumpet with the last days (Matt 24:29-31 echoing Is 27:12-13 and Zech 9:14).

And then the sign of the Son of Man will appear in the sky, and then all the tribes of the earth will mourn, and they will see the Son of Man coming on the clouds of the sky with power and great glory. And He will send forth His angels with a great trumpet and they will gather together His elect from the four winds, from one end of the sky to the other. Matt 24:30-31

Paul had more revelation about this great day. At the sounding of the last (or great) trump the dead shall be raised, and the Lord will gather His elect to Himself.

Behold, I tell you a mystery; we will not all sleep, but we will all be changed, in a moment, in the twinkling of an eye, at the last trumpet; for the trumpet will sound, and the dead will be raised imperishable, and we will be changed. 1 Cor 15:51-52

September

For this we say to you by the word of the Lord, that we who are alive and remain until the coming of the Lord, will not precede those who have fallen asleep. For the Lord Himself will descend from heaven with a shout, with the voice of the archangel and with the trumpet of God, and the dead in Christ will rise first. Then we who are alive and remain will be caught up together with them in the clouds to meet the Lord in the air, and so we shall always be with the Lord. 1 Thess 4:15-17

Photo Lawrence Hirsch

In the book of Revelation, there are seven trumpet judgements. As the final trumpet is sounded:

... there were loud voices in heaven, saying, 'The kingdom of the world has become the kingdom of our Lord and of His Christ; and He will reign forever and ever.' Rev 11:15

We can see the connection between this festival and the coming of the Lord. What a glorious day it will be, and we are to be actively watching and waiting for this day. The trumpets in Israel were silent for nearly 2,000 years but once again they are being sounded, not only by the Jews but also by the prophetic Christians who are sounding the alarm to prepare for His return and declaring the decrees of the Lord over the earth. Furthermore, if we are to be ready for the Lord's wedding day with His bride and coronation as king, we need to be in the right attire at the dress rehearsal ('mo'ed' – appointed time) of which this is one.

Feast of Trumpets – Kathleen Mitchell 2017

All Jewish holidays present us with an opportunity to reassess the course

All Israel Shall be Saved

we've taken in life. The holiday that initiates the Jewish civil calendar, Rosh Hashanah (Head of the Year), clearly sends out a clarion call for personal inventory, to facilitate breakthroughs through a fresh start. It sets the stage for the deep repentance on Yom Kippur, by beginning the introspective Ten Days of Awe. Rosh Hashanah declares a new beginning that will give rise to blessing from YHVH (G-d), wherever the necessary course corrections are made during our second chances.

The day of Rosh Hashanah has historically been a day of breakthrough. It's the anniversary of creation, the date Noah's ark was opened up, and when Joseph was released from Pharaoh's prison. It's a day of hope and opportunity, where struggles are overcome. However, if we are to break through to new blessings, wholeness and maturity, we must begin by looking on the interior, looking back to see where we have missed the mark. If we don't, how will we avoid making the same mistakes again? Being biased in our self-view, we need the Holy Spirit to shine His light of truth, eradicating our self-protective blindness and ignorance. Sitting with an open heart before the Lord, we will see where we have been apathetic, self-indulgent, lazy, compromised, dishonest, rebellious, prideful, disingenuous, unforgiving etc. YHVH will reveal where we have been practising sin or flirting with it, where we have been ignoring the warnings or making excuses for rejecting correction. Too often we've been tolerant of the moral impurity of the world around us and thus participated in it. Perhaps we've refused to step up to the moral high ground because it's unpopular or too costly. These things cannot continue if blessings and breakthroughs are to be ours.

The blowing of the shofar (trumpet) is integral to the observance of Rosh Hashanah. The shofar represents the voice of YHVH. It is a wake-up call. It's a warning to stop walking according to the flesh. It's a call to repentance through awareness of where we line up with the way, will, and word of YHVH. While we eat honey on this holiday to prophesy sweetness to the New Year, the Hebrew word for 'bee' has the same letter order as the 'word' of God. Surely if we are to taste the sweetness of breakthroughs, we will need to base our changes on His word, not upon human ideas. Let's listen to the voice of the Lord, and follow His leading this year.

September

Kathleen D. Mitchell is a 'completed Jew' who is a co-founder of In the Cleft of the Rock Ministries International. She raises up intercessors, leads governmental intercession with the Capitol Hill Prayer Partners in Washington DC, and is involved with 'Intercessors for Israel' in Jerusalem.

The Days of Awe

The Jewish people have a very healthy respect for God as King of the Universe. Many prayers begin with this expression and He is honoured at every Shabbat. On Rosh HaShanah, Psalm 47 is read in the synagogues, a psalm of declaring and crowning God as King and sovereign over all the earth. During this time, Jews attempt to right every wrong and repay every debt. They will ask forgiveness of any they feel they have wronged and try to restore broken relationships. They will also seek to get right with God. What a wonderful season this is – to come before our Heavenly Judge and allow Him to remove the spiritual rubbish in our lives and cleanse us anew. Repentance allows Him to come and fill us deeper with His presence so our joy overflows.

Days of Awe – Jonathan Cahn 2012

The Days of Awe hold a unique place in the Jewish year, and prophetically, in the age...God has set up this entire age as a Hebrew year. As the Hebrew year opened with Passover, so too, the age opened with the Passover of Messiah's death. Then came the Feast of Shavuot or Pentecost, when the Spirit fell on the first believers and finally the summer harvest, the Harvest of salvation. The gospel went out from Jerusalem to the ends of the earth and the Jewish people also went out to the ends of the earth. And so the Age must close with the regathering of the Jewish people to Israel and Jerusalem - to meet the Lord. It is happening before our eyes - as the prophets said. So be not caught sleeping or distracted but stay awake, sober, and on the alert.

All Israel Shall be Saved

The Days of Awe call the children of Israel to get right with God, as preparing for the Day of Judgment. So throughout the ages, the Jewish people have observed the Days of Awe with great reverence and with repentance in getting right with God and man, in forgiving and asking forgiveness, in making amends, in making things right and in tying up the loose ends of life.

For all of us there will come a Day of Judgment and eternity. Therefore these days on earth are the Days of Awe. The days of eternity do not determine your days on earth - but in your days on earth you do determine the days of eternity. Use these days wisely for they come only once in an eternity. Stop compromising. Do what you need to do. Repent, rise up and fulfil the calling God has given you.

Jonathan Cahn is the Senior Pastor and Rabbi of the Jerusalem Center/Beth Israel in Wayne, New Jersey. He also leads the world outreach 'Hope of the World'. He is the author of the New York Times Bestseller, The Harbinger: The Ancient Mystery that Holds the Secret of the World's Future and other books. See Resources.

Yom Kippur – Day of Atonement - 10th Day of Tishrei

Yom Kippur or the Day of Atonement (literally Day of Covering [our sin]) is the holiest day of the entire Hebrew calendar. It is a day of complete fasting from both food and water, and in Israel nothing but emergency vehicles (and children's bikes and skateboards) move on the roads. All shops are shut and the nation comes to an eerie hush as people walk to the overflowing synagogues for a day-long ritual of repentance. Leviticus chapter 16 sets out the biblical requirements for the day's proceedings. The High Priest was to enter the Holy of Holies on this one day only to atone for his own sin, for the temple and for the sins of the nation by the shedding of blood.

September

As there is no longer a temple, there is a problem for the Jewish people. The rabbis have replaced the biblical requirements with good deeds of charity (mitzvoth), repentance (teshuva), and prayer, but these can never atone for sin.

However, a sacrifice has been made which does atone for sin – Yeshua the Messiah, as the book of Hebrews makes clear:

But when Christ appeared as a high priest of the good things to come, He entered through the greater and more perfect tabernacle, not made with hands, that is to say, not of this creation; and not through the blood of goats and calves, but through His own blood, He entered the holy place once for all, having obtained eternal redemption. Heb 9:11-12

Two goats were brought to the High Priest on Yom Kippur as sin offerings for the people (Lev 16:5,8). The High Priest drew a lot to decide which one would be sacrificed and its blood sprinkled on the mercy seat, and on which he would lay his hands on its head transferring the sins of the nation symbolically to it, then sent it outside the camp into the desert as the 'Azazel' scapegoat, never to return (Lev 16:10,15,20-22). At the trial before the crucifixion, Jesus was presented to the High Priest,  then sacrificed while another Jesus (according to several ancient gospel texts) called Barabbas, meaning 'son of the father', was set free!

In both the Jerusalem (Jacob Neusner, The Yerushalmi, p.156-157) and the Babylonian (Soncino version, Yoma 39b) versions of the Talmud (rabbinic commentary on the Jewish Scriptures), it is recorded that on Yom Kippur, a red cord was tied around the doors of the Temple which would sometimes miraculously turn white, indicating that the sins of the nation were forgiven. This had happened for the 200 years before 30 CE, but for the 40 years

All Israel Shall be Saved

before the destruction of the temple in 70 CE, it never happened. This is the time of the death and resurrection of Yeshua. The same passage also says that the doors of the Temple which were shut each night, opened of their own accord each morning, the western Menorah would not stay alight and the lot for the Lord (goat for sacrifice) always came up in the left hand. The statistical chances of this are about 1:5.5 billion. God gave the Jewish people clear signs that the old means of sacrifice were no longer necessary and that the way into the holy place was now to be open for all to enter. http://www3.telus.net/public/kstam/en/temple/details/evidence.htm

The blood of bulls and goats could never take away sin (Heb 10:3-4), only cover it, but the blood of the Lamb of God did far more: it washed sin away as if it never existed (Ps 103:1, 1 Jn 1:9). *He who knew no sin was made sin on our behalf, that we might become the righteousness of God in Him* (2 Cor 5:21). Every 50 years, the Year of Jubilee was proclaimed by the shofar sound immediately after Yom Kippur ended, announcing the restoration of property and freedom from slavery (Lev 25:9ff).

Prophetically, this day looks forward toward the day when Israel will recognise her Messiah as the one whom they have pierced and weep bitterly (Zech 12:10, Matt 24:30, Rev 1:7).

I will pour out on the house of David and on the inhabitants of Jerusalem, the Spirit of grace and of supplication, so that they will look on Me whom they have pierced; and they will mourn for Him, as one mourns for an only son, and they will weep bitterly over Him like the bitter weeping over a firstborn. Zech 12:10

God revealed Himself to one Jewish lady in the synagogue on Yom Kippur. As the rabbi preached about the sacrifices, she saw Yeshua behind him on the cross. He *was* the *sacrificial* lamb that the rabbi was describing! She spoke to Him and said that she knew in her heart He could take away sin and He replied that He *had* taken it away. He then gave her an open-heart operation, only without the pain, in which He took away her sin and gave her a new clean heart...When she left the synagogue, her life was transformed.

September

She *knew* her sins were forgiven and that her name *was* written in the Book of Life.

Feast of Tabernacles/Booths – Sukkot – Feast of Ingathering, Lev 23:33-43, Ex 23:16

The Feast of Tabernacles is so named because it remembers the wilderness wandering of the Hebrew people in the desert for 40 years. The people were commanded to build booths (temporary shelters) and to eat and sleep in them for seven days to graphically remind them that earth is not their eternal home, only a temporary dwelling place. It is celebrated on the 15th day of Tishrei and the command was to rejoice because the work of gathering in the fruit harvest was now complete. As specified in Leviticus 23:39-40, the tabernacles were to be constructed of palm branches, willows, fruit of beautiful trees (etrog – a citrus, like a large lemon) and boughs of leafy trees (myrtle). Today the four species are bound together in a 'lulav'. If there is no lawn space for a Sukkah, they are often built on balconies.

Yeshua visited Jerusalem for the Feast of Tabernacles recorded in John chapter 7. One of the rituals carried out at the time of Jesus was the 'water libation ceremony' where the priests daily drew water from the pool of Siloam in a golden pitcher, brought it up to the Temple and poured it out at the foot of the altar, praying for rain (Is 12:3). No doubt, Jesus and His disciples were watching this and He took the opportunity to proclaim:

Now on the last day, the great day of the feast, Jesus stood and cried out, saying, "If anyone is thirsty, let him come to Me and drink. He who believes in Me, as the Scripture said, 'From his innermost being will flow rivers of living water.'" John 7:37-38

All Israel Shall be Saved

At that time in the temple, large menorot (plural of menorah - lampstand) were lit in the temple precincts to give light for the festival. It would have been an impressive sight visible from far away and guiding the pilgrims to the city. In John chapter 8, Jesus said:

Then Jesus again spoke to them, saying, "I am the Light of the world; he who follows Me will not walk in the darkness, but will have the Light of life." John 8:12

The tabernacles reminded the people that God never deserted them during their forty years in the desert but always provided for them. He guided them with a cloud by day and a pillar of fire by night and He dwelt among them. So today, He still dwells amongst us (Jn 1:14) and in the kingdom to come, He promises:

The tabernacle of God is amongst men, and He will dwell with them and they shall be His people...and God will wipe away every tear from their eyes. There shall be no more death, nor sorrow, nor crying. There shall be no more pain for the former things have passed away. Rev 21:3,4

The Feast of Tabernacles is also the festival of the nations. The rabbis say the 70 sacrifices made at Sukkot (Num 29:13f) represented the 70 nations of the world established in Genesis 10 (Sukkah 55b). It is a representative number for all nations. In future times, the fallen tabernacle of David will be restored (Amos 9:11-12), the final harvest will be brought in (Ex 23:16,

34:22) and during the Messianic reign all nations must come up to Jerusalem to worship the Lord. If they refuse, there will be dire consequences.

And it shall come to pass that everyone who is left of all the nations which come against Jerusalem shall go up from year

to year to worship the King, the Lord of Hosts and to keep the Feast of Tabernacles... and if they don't they will have no rain. Zech 14:16-17

Thank the Lord that since 1980, when the International Christian Embassy in Jerusalem began to hold a conference, delegates from many nations have come prophetically to bless Israel and their own countries by their participation. This was started to counter the decision of the world's embassies to move out of Jerusalem in protest to Israel's declaration of Jerusalem as the undivided capital of Israel. In His time, the nations will all learn the ways of the Lord and there will be peace on earth.

Now it will come about that in the last days the mountain of the house of the LORD will be established as the chief of the mountains...and all the nations will stream to it. And many peoples will come and say, Come, let us go up to the mountain of the LORD, to the house of the God of Jacob; that He may teach us concerning His ways and that we may walk in His paths.' For the law will go forth from Zion and the word of the LORD from Jerusalem. And He will judge between the nations, and will render decisions for many peoples; and they will hammer their swords into plowshares and their spears into pruning hooks. Nation will not lift up sword against nation, and never again will they learn war. Isaiah 2:2-4

Most likely, the transfiguration happened at Sukkot as Peter was asking if he should build tabernacles for Moses, Elijah and Jesus (Matt 17:1-8). Solomon's temple was also dedicated at this time of year (2 Chron 7:1-10) and Nehemiah's spiritual revival occurred during Sukkot (Neh 8:13-18).

Feast of Tabernacles – Daniel Nissim 2011

Of all Biblical holy days, Sukkot (Feast of Tabernacles) is in some ways the most exciting and meaningful. Sukkot commemorates the days in which our forefathers dwelt in the wilderness in tents and temporary dwellings. Paradoxically, the Creator of the Universe also chose to make his abode a 'Tabernacle' as well! Thus, we had good company – the Presence of The Name – leading us and coming with us in the pillar of fire and the pillar of

All Israel Shall be Saved

cloud that were ever above His Holy Place (Ex 40:34-38).

No more reason than this is required for us to call Sukkot the 'Season of our Joy'. In Jewish communities around the world, as soon as Yom Kippur is over, temporary shelters are erected. In colder climates such as England, they are often built well enough to put a heater in. Ideally, at least one meal a day is eaten outdoors in the 'Sukkah'. The religious walk to and fro from synagogue, carrying their 'lulavs' to wave before the L-rd.

Sukkah

Based on the four species mentioned in Leviticus 23:40, the lulav has four plants. First, there is a citron, which we call an 'etrog'. With a taste similar to that of the bark of the tree it is from, it reminds us of the tree of the knowledge of good and evil from which we were commanded not to eat (Gen 2:17). The palm branch, straight as an arrow, reminds us of the need to be upright as a palm. A few sprigs of myrtle, whose leaves are shaped like the human eye, remind us of wisdom and enlightenment, and a few sprigs of willow, which droop down, remind us of how we ought to be humble and contrite in prayer before the Holy One.

What a wonderful picture Sukkot is for us today! Just as G-d was with Israel in the wilderness, so was His Son with us in the person of Yeshua who dwelt (literally 'tabernacled') among us (John 1:14). Just as Israel saw the Glory of G-d in the wilderness, so we saw His Glory in and through Yeshua. Indeed, this is the season when Yeshua takes his seat upon the throne of His ancestor David, that all the nations will come to worship Him year by year in Jerusalem (Ezek 37:24; Zech 14:16). What a glorious day that will be!

September

Dr Daniel Nessim is the leader of Kehillath Tsion in Vancouver and the Seattle director for Chosen People Ministries. He and his wife Deborah have three children and two grandchildren.

September Prayer Points – The Feasts

1. Pray for an awe of God Almighty to fall over the people. Ex 15:11
2. Repent before a Holy God, the Judge of all the earth. Pray that He will show us where we've become comfortable with rebellion. Ps 96:7-13, 1 Sam 15:23
3. Pray for Israel to hear the call to return to their God (Hos 3:4-5). Pray for revival among God's people throughout the world and salvation in the end-time harvest. Ps 85:8-13
4. As the Jewish and Gentile believers gather in Jerusalem at this time, may they be a sweet fragrance of Yeshua to the lost. 2 Cor 2:14-15
5. Pray that we will all use this season through prayer and repentance to ready ourselves for the Bridegroom's return (Rev 19:7). Pray that He will show us where we've avoided seeking His assessments. Gen 3:8-10
6. As the shofars sound, pray for Israel to hear the voice of the Lord. Ex 19:15-19, 20:20-23
7. Proclaim the shofar call to the Jewish people to gather to their God. Is 27:12-13
8. Prepare your heart through this time also. Pray that He will show us where we've pridefully ignored His warnings. Ps 51
9. Pray for the shofar to awaken Israel and the church from slumber to recognise the days in which we live and be ready for Yeshua's return. Matt 24:42-51
10. Pray that God will hasten the day when the Jewish people shall look upon Him, and find the fountain which is open for sin and uncleanness. Zech 12:10, 13:1
11. Pray for protection from attacks in the physical and spiritual realm. In 1973, Israel was attacked on Yom Kippur. Ps 121
12. Pray for the evil of sin to be revealed to Israel and the church and true repentance to come forth, not rituals or pride. Joel 2:12-20, Jer 17:9-10, Matt chapter 23

13. Give thanks for the atonement we have through Yeshua by His grace, not our works. Heb 9:11-16
14. Ponder the righteous judgement of God. Rev 3:1-6, 20:11-15
15. Pray for the Jews to recognise that forgiveness has been won and is available now in Yeshua. Acts 10:40-43, Acts 2:37-39
16. For the congregations in Israel to boldly share the good news with their fellow countrymen. 1 Cor 15:13-20
17. May Israelis understand how they can be assured their names are written in the Lamb's Book of Life. Rev 3:5, 21:27
18. For revival in Israel and the success of Jewish outreach ministries worldwide. Ps 85:1-7
19. Pray for the veil to be removed from the eyes of the Jewish people so they can see clearly the way of salvation and put their faith in Yeshua. 2 Cor 3:15, Is 63:15-17, Rom 10:1
20. Pray for them to understand that no amount of good deeds can remove sin – only blood can wash them clean (Lev 17:11) and only the blood of Yeshua has been shed for sin. Heb 9:18-28
21. Pray for more dreams, visions and revelations of the Lamb of God in the synagogues. Jn 1:29
22. Pray for good physical and spiritual rain during spring, winter and autumn rain as this is the beginning of the wet season. Lev 26:3-5
23. Pray for the thirsty to come and drink the Living Water. Jn 4:13-15, 7:37
24. Pray for Israel to dwell with God during Sukkot. Ezek 43:7
25. Pray that we would all focus on what is of eternal importance, not temporal things. 1 Cor 3:10-15
26. Rejoice in the presence of the Lord and thank him for his abundant provision. Lev 23:40, Phil 4:4
27. Pray for workers for the gathering in of the final harvest of souls. Matt 13:39, 41-43, Matt 24:13, Ps 126:5-6
28. Pray for Israel to recognise that Jesus is the only true Light of the World, and to come to the Light of life. Jn 8:12
29. Pray that those from the nations visiting for the High Holiday festivals will be a joyful witness to the Jewish people and have opportunities to share Yeshua, the Jewish Messiah. Is 12:2-6
30. For a great harvest amongst the Jewish people this Sukkot. Jn 4:34-38

October

Prophesying Life to the Dry Bones

Photo courtesy Lawrence Hirsch

Pure and undefiled religion in the sight of our God and Father is this: to visit orphans and widows in their distress, and to keep oneself unstained by the world. James 1:27

And the Word became flesh, and dwelt among us, and we saw His glory, glory as of the only begotten from the Father, full of grace and truth. John 1:14

Then He said to me, 'Prophesy to the breath, prophesy, son of man, and say to the breath, "Thus says the Lord GOD, 'Come from the four winds, O breath, and breathe on these slain, that they come to life.'" Ezek 37:9

October

God commanded Ezekiel to prophesy before the bones could come together and the breath of life could come into the dead bones. We are an integral part of God's revival plan. This month we will look at the final feast days, then turn our attention to the ministries in the land and be prophesying over Israel's dry bones.

Global Day of Prayer for the Peace of Jerusalem - First Sunday in October

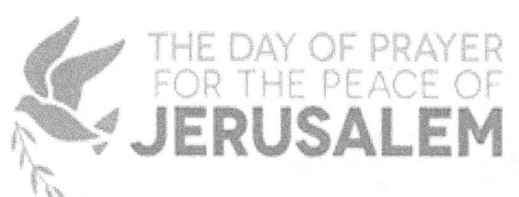

The Global Day of Prayer for the Peace of Jerusalem is commemorated each year on the first Sunday in October, near the season of Yom Kippur. It was initially called in 2002 by a very reputable team of leaders in the US headed by Dr Jack Hayford (The Church on the Way) and Rev Rob Stearns (Eagles' Wings Ministries) and has quickly become the largest Israel-focused prayer event in the world with hundreds of millions joining across the world. It aims to raise global awareness and intercession for God's purposes in Israel, and to unite believers in raising a cry to Heaven on behalf of this strategic land and its people. *The Jewish and Israel Prayer Focus* is pleased to be a part of this worldwide call. The call to prayer for Jerusalem is based on the following four tenets.

- *Understanding*...that we are children of Abraham by faith, the 'wild olive branch' grafted in to the root of God's covenant (Romans 11:17-26)
- *Recognizing*...that God has kept his word to Abraham and His descendents and settled them in their homeland again, according to the word of the prophets (Amos 9:14-15, Ezekiel chapter 36, especially v 24)
- *Recognizing*...that we have a biblical mandate according to Psalm 122 and many other Scriptures to seek the good and prosperity of Jerusalem

All Israel Shall be Saved

until the Lord makes her a praise in all the earth
- *Affirming*...that God's love and intended blessing is for all nations and peoples, and that we have goodwill and love for all mankind, including all inhabitants of the Holy Land, and desire the peace of this entire region.

Dr Hayford states, 'We are living in a sobering moment in history that calls us, as people of God to fulfill our biblical mandate to pray for the peace of Jerusalem, and to stand against the alarming rise of anti-Semitism. We are not to be passive; we are called to pray with passion, to intercede. This is not about politics; this is about the Word of God.'

It is suggested that we pray the following prayer and proclaim the Scriptures noted.

> Our Father in heaven, the God of Abraham, Isaac, and Jacob, in obedience to Your Word, I pray for the peace of Jerusalem and the Land of Israel. Bless the people of Israel with Your promise of redemption, shield them with your love, and bring them renewed hope for their day of salvation. Guide Israel's leaders and advisors with the light of Your truth. For Your Name's sake, I ask that You remember Your promise and bless the Land with peace, and its inhabitants with lasting joy.

Scriptures to Proclaim: Ps 122:6-8, Is 40:1-2, 62:1,6-7, Amos 9:11,14-15, Rom 11:1-2a,b, Zech 8:2-3, Deut 10:14-15.

Other scriptures to read: Deut chapter 10, Is 60:10-22, Zech chapter 12, Rom chapter 11, Heb chapter 11, Isaiah chapter 62, Ezek chapter 37, 39:25-29, Mic 7:18-20

You are encouraged to organise a special service, prayer meeting or display to raise awareness of God's purposes for Israel and join with the global community praying in unison on this day. You can find more information and resources on the website: http://www.daytopray.com

October

The Final Feasts: Hoshana Rabbah and Shemini Atzeret

The Great Hosannah is commemorated on the 7th day of Sukkot, almost always in October. The Hallel psalms are recited (Ps 113-118). In the Temple on the final day, the Messianic expectation climaxed with the recitation of Ps 118:25-26 and palm branches were waved to greet the Messiah:

'O Lord do save, we beseech you, do save we beseech you, do send prosperity', Blessed is the one who comes in the name of the LORD; We have blessed you from the house of the LORD.

Shemini Atzeret means gathering or assembly of the eighth. The only biblical instructions or information given is that it is to be a holy convocation and there were to be offerings by fire to the Lord (Lev 23:36,39, Num 29:35-38). The 8th day was the day the covenant of circumcision was enacted (Gen 17:9-14). When Solomon's temple was dedicated in 1 Kgs 8:2, the glory filled the temple and on the eighth day, the people blessed the king and went away joyfully (v 66). The 8th day is also the first day of the new beginning, a new  week or a new era and, as such, prophetically the eternal kingdom. It speaks of the new heavens and the new earth foretold in Rev 21:1-5.

Simchat Torah - Rejoicing in the Eternal Word of God

In modern times, on the last day of the Feast, there is a non-biblical tradition that began in the Middle Ages, called 'Simchat Torah', which means 'rejoicing in the Law'. Today, these three celebrations are often celebrated together. Simchat Torah occurs at the point where the weekly readings from the Torah (Pentateuch) finish and the new cycle begins. It celebrates the joy in the instructions of God given to Moses. The scrolls are paraded around the synagogue and even out into the streets with much joyful dancing and singing. The Torah scrolls are the most precious possession of most synagogues and Jews have often died to protect them. However, it is sad that the interpretations of the rabbis are now more studied than the Word itself and given equal status. Pray that they will return to seek God to reveal truth to them personally.

For believers, the Word has now been made flesh and dwelt among us in person (Jn 1:14). Whilst Yeshua did not come to abolish the Law or the Prophets, He did come to fulfil them (Matt 5:17). Now both Jews and Gentiles are made righteous, not through the Law but through faith in Yeshua the Messiah (Rom 3:28-31). May we all delight in the law of the Lord as King David did and meditate on it day and night (Ps 1:2).

Now we turn to the living stones in the land and see how the Lord is moving in Messianic ministries throughout the Land.

Fellowship of Israel-Related Ministries - Ann Hilsden 2018

My husband, Wayne, and I arrived in Israel in the summer of 1983 with two toddlers. We were young, ill-equipped, quite ignorant, but very keen to see what God would unfold in spite of our lack of qualifications. Our main goal that first year was planting a congregation with another couple that preceded us, learning the language and culture and meeting the people.

Thirty five years later we look back and see that miracle after miracle has been the pattern of growth. King of Kings Community has been a strong

October

congregation of several hundred for the past 25 years, bringing in and sending out. Local congregations have been planted in other languages, and under King of Kings, Israel College of the Bible began in 1990. God has provided amazing facilities in the heart of Jerusalem where thirteen different congregations meet at various times, plus food and clothing are given to the poor. The Anchor of Hope counselling centre is there for the hurting, and the Yuval School of Music and the Arts provides training for almost 200 students who want to use their talents for the Lord! Almost three years ago my husband passed on the baton of leadership to a younger man, Chad Holland, who is capably leading the ministry forward.

Months before that, my husband officially launched the Fellowship of Israel Related Ministries (FIRM), a Global network which exists to inspire, engage, and connect people around the world with what God is doing in Israel. Within Israel we have over sixty ministries that are vetted as a part of our network. We help these ministries tell their stories and in doing so, visitors to Israel are impacted in a powerful way. FIRM holds events throughout the year, which we call 'FIRM Handshakes' for pastors and leaders, and we have done this in over a dozen major cities including London, Ottawa, Singapore, Paris, Chicago, and shortly in Cape Town. It is an open conversation in hopes of engaging the unengaged. We also speak in colleges and universities to help young people sort through the issues about Israel.

In addition to the many specialised tours that FIRM facilitates throughout the year, one of the main tools of engagement is our annual conference, the Jerusalem Encounter – to encounter God, the Land and the people, especially the 'living stones'. Hundreds of young people, including pastors, leaders, and educators come to Israel for the first time for this tour and conference. Let His Kingdom come. https://firm.org.il

----

The FIRM website lists many Messianic organisations in Israel. Another excellent website is Kehila News Israel https://app.kehila.org/ministries

which lists 87 ministries in Israel plus other lists such as congregations, schools, businesses etc. From the following list, it is suggested that you choose a few in an area that touches your heart, make contact with them and pray regularly for them.

Ministries in Israel

Arad

> Ark in the Negev – substance abuse rehab (women) – Polly Sigulim 2012 http://www.arkinthenegev.com

Ashdod

- Voice of Judah – humanitarian aid, evangelism, church planting – Israel Pochtar, Jacques Van Der Merwe (International coordinator) 2008 vojisrael.intl@gmail.com https://vojisrael.org
- Yeshuat Ami Ministries – outreach and prayer – Simcha and Bella Davidov 2013 https://yeshuatami.com/about

Beer Sheva

- Aviv Ministries – alcoholic and drug addiction recovery - Dov Bikas 2014 https://www.avivministry.com/en
- Final Frontier Ministries – worship centre and evangelism – Avner and Rachel Boskey 2002, 2003, 2009, 2011 https://davidstent.org
- Simeon's Cry – Humanitarian aid and evangelism – Sean & Ayelet Steckbeck 2008 http://simeonscry.org
- Streams in the Desert – humanitarian aid to orphans and single mums and their children – Mariana Gol 2017, 2018 http://streamsinthedesert.co
- Streams of Hope – humanitarian aid – Dmitri Brodkin (no English) – Ya'akov and Carla koosbouterse@gmail.com (English contacts) 2014, 2016

October

Eilat

Eilat Shelter Hostel – a backpackers' hostel and Messianic congregation – John and Judy Pex info@shelterhostel.com, http://www.shelterhostel.com

Haifa/Mt Carmel

- Acharit v'Tikvah (A Future and a Hope) – pregnancy counseling – Marvin Kramer 2010 jer_29:11@netvision.net.il, https://afutureandahope.org.il
- Christian Soldiers' Ministry – supporting Arab Christians (and others) in the IDF – Najeeb and Elizabeth Atteih 2019
- Ebenezer Home for the Messianic Elderly 2010 info@ebenezer.co.il https://www.ebenezer.co.il
- Hadar HaCarmel (Glory of Carmel) – humanitarian aid, outreach, discipleship – Ps Vladamir Tsapar 2016 https://www.carmelcongregation.org.il/ministries/hadar-hacarmel-center
- House of Victory – drug and alcohol rehabilitation (men) – Eric Benson 2007 houseofv@netvision.net.il, https://www.carmelcongregation.org.il/ministries/house-victory
- Ima's Goodies – ministry to soldiers – Renee Shmuel 2016 https://www.imasgoodies.com
- Out of Zion Ministries – prayer and aliya ministry – David and Josie Silver 2004, 2011, 2015 http://www.out-of-zion.com
- Or HaCarmel Shelter – refuge for mothers, especially Sudanese refugees – Rita Tsukahira 2012 https://www.carmelcongregation.org.il/ministries/womens-shelter
- Shavei Tzion (Return to Zion) – music classes, media ministry (Russian), Holocaust survivors, new immigrants, soldiers humanitarian aid and support – Leon Mazin 2016 info@shaveitzion.org, http://english.shaveitzion.org

Jericho

Seeds of Hope – Humanitarian aid to Palestinians – Khader Ghanim (Tass Saada founder), 2013 https://seedsofhope.org

All Israel Shall be Saved

Jerusalem

- Anchor of Hope – counselling assistance and training – Dr Katherine Snyder 2019 http://anchorofhope.org.il
- Be'ad Chaim – Pro life, Israel – pregnancy counselling and anti-abortion ministry – Sandy Shoshani 2004, 2015 info@beadchaim.org.il https://www.beadchaim.com
- Beit HaYeshua – drug and alcohol rehabilitation – Zvi Randelman 2012 http://beithayeshua.org/home.html
- Bible Society in Israel – Victor Kalisher 2013 info@biblesocietyinisrael.com https://biblesocietyinisrael.com
- Caspari Centre for Biblical and Jewish Studies – Lisa Loden 2004 training@caspari.com https://www.caspari.com
- Chazon Yerushalayim (Jerusalem Vision) – evangelism, discipleship, reconciliation – Shmuel and Pamela Suran 2010 http://jerusalemvision.com
- Emet Zion Music – music ministry – Micha'el and Ashley Ben David 2017 https://emetzionmusic.com
- Fellowship of Israel-Related Ministries – connecting churches to Israeli congregations and ministries – Wayne and Ann Hilsden 2018 http://firm.org.il
- For Zion's Sake Ministry – humanitarian aid – Brad Antolovich https://forzion.com
- The Golden Report – aliya – Jerry Golden 2012 https://thegoldenreport.net
- HaTikvah Project (hope) – dentistry, child adoption – Evan Levine 2016, 2019 https://hatikvaproject.org
- Hebrew People – teaching and discipleship – Martie Nel 2006 https://hebrewpeople.com
- Highway 19 Ministries – reconciliation, Syrian relief, leadership training – Steve Carpenter 2015 http://www.highway19.org
- Hope for Israel – youth, discipleship, humanitarian aid – Moran Rosenblit 2010 iladmin@hope4israel.org, https://hope4israel.org/who-we-are
- Jamie Cowen Ministries – teacher – Jamie Cowen 2017 http://www.jamiecowenministries.com
- Jill Shannon – music and teaching 2013, 2019 http://coffeetalkswithmessiah.com

October

- Jerusalem Institute of Justice – legal aid for Messianic Jews and others – Calev Myers 2009 http://www.jij.org
- Keren Ha Shlichut – Israeli missions to the nations – Gavriel Gefen 2005, 2006, 2011, 2016 https://www.shlichut.net (in Hebrew so you will need the translation tool)
- Mekor HaTikvah Messianic School – Colin Ross 2009 makor@013.net http://www.makorhatikvah.org
- Michel Rebiai – reconciliation, evangelism 2009 www.gdv-cor-ch (in German) https://app.kehila.org/community-of-reconciliation
- One for Israel Bible College – Messianic Bible College – Erez Soref 2003 https://college.oneforisrael.org
- Revive Israel Ministries – evangelism and discipleship training – Asher and Betty Intrater 2003, 2004, 2011 https://www.reviveisrael.org/about-us
- The Sheba Foundation – assisting Ethiopian immigrants – Jennifer Kaplan 2004, 2016 http://sheba.org.il
- Shevet Achim – life-saving heart operations for Palestinian children in Israeli hospitals – Jonathan Miles 2005, 2018 https://www.shevet.org
- Tikkun International – restoration of Israel and Jewish-Gentile reconciliation – Dan Juster 2005 info@tikkuninternational.org, https://tikkun.tv
- Vision for Israel/Joseph Storehouse – humanitarian aid – Barry and Batya Segal 2002, 2006, 2016 info@visionforisrael.com, https://www.visionforisrael.com/en
- Yedidiya Centre – preparing youth for IDF duty – Michael and Rachel Relf 2017 yedidyacentre@gmail.com
- Yuval School of Music and the Arts 2017 Yuval.artschool@hotmail.com, https://yuvalarts.org

Kadesh Barnea

Yad Ohevet – House of Refuge – Avishai and Jolanda Pinchas 2010, 2017

Karmiel

Rivers of Living Water – humanitarian aid, outreach 2004 rolw@012.net.il https://rolwisrael.org

All Israel Shall be Saved

Kiryat Jearim

>Yad HaShmonah – Messianic community – Gershon Nerel 2015 https://www.yadha8.co.il/en

Netanya

>Abundant Bread of Salvation – humanitarian aid centre – Brian and Racheli Slater (and Tel Aviv) 2011 http://yeshuasfreshbreadinisrael.blogspot.com https://www.facebook.com/AbundantBreadOfSalvation

Nazareth

>Fellowship of Christian Students – discipleship and missions – Zahar Haddad 2002, 2014 info@fcsi.ws, http://en.fcsi.ws

Petach Tikvah

>Lech Lecha – discipleship ministry – Liah Lavie 2018 https://www.lechlcha.com

Rishon L'Zion

>Awake Israel Ministries – evangelism and teaching – Shlomy and Miriam Abramov 2011, 2018 http://awakeisrael.org

Sderot

- Hands of Mercy – humanitarian aid – Yariv Goldman 2018 http://www.israel-handsofmercy.org
- Hope for Sderot – humanitarian aid – Stewart Ganulin 2012 http://www.hopeforsderot.com

October

Shefa Amer

King's Kids – children's ministry for Jewish and Arab children – Rajaa' and Alon Grimberg 2019 http://houseoflight.net/king-s-kids/index.php/about

Tiberias/Poriya

- Aliyah Return Center – aliya, settling new immigrants – Chaim Malespin 2014 watchaliyah@gmail.com, https://www.aliyahreturncenter.com
- Beit Bracha – Messianic guest house, prayer and retreat centre – Ted Walker (Magdala) https://www.cmj-israel.org/beit-bracha
- Daniel Carmel – music ministry and boat captain 2014 http://www.seaofgalileeworshipboats.com
- Emmaus Way – evangelism, prayer and worship ministry – Arni and Yonit Klein 2002, 2013, 2015 https://www.emmausway.org
- Heart of G-d Ministries – church planting, music and evangelism – Richard and Carolyn Hyde 2010, 2018 https://heartofg-d.org
- The Galilee Experience – multimedia evangelism and business – Eric Morey 2003 http://www.thegalileeexperience.com/shop/about_us

Tel Aviv/Jaffa/Kfar Saba

- Chaim Beshefa (Abundant life) – pregnancy counselling – Anat and Ishai Brenner 2009, 2013 chaimbeshefa@gmail.com, http://www.abundantlife.org.il
- Chosen People Ministries Israel – evangelism – Michael Z. https://www.chosenpeople.com/site/cpm-israel
- Messiah's Mandate – teacher – Ron Cantor 2013 http://messiahsmandate.org
- Ot U'Mofet (Sign and a Wonder) – ministry to widows and orphans – Orna Greenman 2013 aleftav@netvision.net.il https://ornagrinman.com
- Trumpet of Salvation – evangelism – Yakov and Elisheva Damkani (and Gilgal Hotel) 2005, 2015 Info@TrumpetofSalvation.org https://trumpetofsalvation.org

All Israel Shall be Saved

October Prayer Points – The Dry Bones

"Son of Man, can these bones live?" And I answered, "O Lord GOD, You know." Again He said to me, "Prophesy over these bones and say to them, 'O dry bones, hear the word of the LORD.' Thus says the Lord GOD to these bones, 'Behold, I will cause breath to enter you that you may come to life. I will put sinews on you, make flesh grow back on you, cover you with skin and put breath in you that you may come alive; and you will know that I am the LORD.'" Ezek 37:3-6

1. *Our bones are dried up and our hope has perished. We are completely cut off* (v 11). Speak hope to the house of Israel that God has not deserted them.
2. *They were very dry* (v 2). Pray especially for the Jews in Muslim countries such as Iran, Syria and Egypt. None is so far from God that He cannot hear when they cry out to Him.
3. *O dry bones, hear the word of the LORD* (v 4). Pray for the deaf ears to be opened to hear God's word.
4. Pray for the prophets in Israel and elsewhere to be raised up to speak God's word.
5. Pray for the secular Jews to hear God's word. Name any you personally know.
6. Pray for those entrenched in Jewish religious traditions to hear God's word.
7. *I will open your graves and cause you to come up out of your graves, My people* (v 12). Speak the word that the dead hearts of flesh will live; the graves will be opened.
8. *As I prophesied, there was a noise, and behold, a rattling; and the bones came together, bone to its bone* (v 7). Pray for God to shake the dead bones, especially those in the US and other Western countries that are too comfortable to want to move.
9. Pray for the bones from across the world to come together to form a united nation in Israel. Pray also for unity for the government which is formed from many factions.

October

10. *I will bring you into the land of Israel* (v 12). Speak prophetically to the Jews in the US, Canada, France, South America, Melbourne, Sydney and elsewhere that they will return. Pray for God to begin to stir their hearts and draw them to Israel.
11. *Then you will know that I am the LORD, when I have opened your graves and caused you to come up out of your graves, My people* (v 13). It is God who causes them to come. Pray for their hearts to be melted by His love.
12. Prophesy that they will know that He is the Lord. Coming back to the land is only the start. His purpose is for them to know God in covenant relationship. Pray for this personal knowledge of Him to increase.
13. *And I looked, and behold, sinews were on them* (v 8). Sinews hold the bones together. Pray for the media and communications to report truth and cause Israel to form strong bonds, not incite division.
14. Pray for the legal system to align with God's Word, not the world's. Pray for compassion and mercy, especially for the believers in Israel who are often not treated justly.
15. Pray for Israel to look to God, not other nations, for its security. Pray for wisdom for its leaders.
16. *And flesh grew* (v 8). Flesh is the muscle that gives strength and flexibility. Pray for the business and economic sector to grow strong, for innovation, creativity and smart ideas.
17. Pray for education and health to be developed according to God's agenda.
18. *and skin covered them* (v 8). Skin protects the inward parts and holds all together. Pray for all those who are protecting Israel – the border security guards and the soldiers.
19. Pray for the police and the secret intelligence services (Shin Bet, Mossad).
20. *but there was no breath in them* (v 8). We can have the appearance of life but not be alive. It is only God that can give life. His presence is what makes the difference. Pray for His presence to hover over Israel as over the waters at creation.
21. *Behold, I will cause breath to enter you that you may come to life* (v 5). Remind God of His promise. He will cause it to happen.
22. *Then He said to me, 'Prophesy to the breath, prophesy, son of man, and say to the breath, "Thus says the Lord GOD, 'Come from the four*

All Israel Shall be Saved

winds, O breath, and breathe on these slain, that they come to life'" (v 9). Call the breath of God to breathe on the slain.
23. Speak life over the priesthood of Israel, namely the rabbis. Pray for visions by day and dreams by night of who the Messiah is.
24. Pray for the secret believers to come out from the closet and boldly share their experiences.
25. Pray for the evangelists to go forth and boldly speak the Word of Truth to the nation.
26. Pray for the pastors to call for repentance and a turning away from sin. Pray that they may not just preach a gospel of good works, but salvation by faith worked out in deed.
27. Pray for God to cleanse the nation with His purifying fires so it may be a righteous nation.
28. *and the breath came into them, and they came to life and stood on their feet, an exceedingly great army* (v 10). Pray for the army of the Lord to rise up and begin training, especially the young believers.
29. Praise God that it will be an exceedingly great army.
30. *"I will put My Spirit within you and you will come to life, and I will place you on your own land. Then you will know that I, the LORD, have spoken and done it," declares the LORD* (v 14). Pray for an outpouring of the Spirit as at Pentecost that will disperse fear and be a mighty witness to the nation and the world.
31. Praise God that all the world will know that God has spoken and He has done it (v 14).

November

Grafted in to the Olive Tree

Garden of Gethsemane

...some of the branches were broken off, and you, being a wild olive, were grafted in among them and became partaker with them of the rich root of the olive tree. Rom 11:17

For He Himself is our peace, who made both groups into one and broke down the barrier of the dividing wall...so that in Himself He might make the two into one new man, thus establishing peace, and might reconcile them both in one body to God through the cross, by it having put to death the enmity. Eph 2:14-16

November

Grafted in

God is calling us to be grafted in to His plans and purposes and we are then to be connected with His covenant people and land. Our destiny as nations must be aligned with Jesus' destiny as King. Jew and Gentile are to work together to bring about God's purposes not separately. Ruth is a classic example of a Gentile who left all to become grafted in to Israel and then God rewarded her with becoming the great-grandmother of King David.

What does it mean to be grafted in today?

• Connecting in prayer

There are many online prayer opportunities, some small home group meetings that pray for Israel and email or post newsletters from ministries to keep you informed. Many of the congregations and ministries have websites and you can sign up for their direct news. These have been given in February or October where they are known. *The Jewish and Israel Prayer Focus* and *Prayer for Israel* have prayer letters focusing on the congregations and ministries which you can sign up for. There are many other Christian Israel-supporting ministries or Jewish organisations that send out newsletters which focus more on political issues or issues of mutual Jewish-Christian interest.

Succat Hallel Prayer House

• Supporting financially

The believers in the land are crying out for material support for their work. Almost every congregation is reaching out to their community through humanitarian aid. However, much Christian support (especially from the

All Israel Shall be Saved

US) is directed through Jewish organisations rather than the believers. This is a shame, as the opportunities to share the gospel with the assistance are then limited. My advice is to support the believers directly through their ministries. *The Jewish and Israel Prayer Focus* works in this way and all donations given to Israeli congregations are passed on directly in full (http://jewishandisraelprayerfocus.org click donate). You can also do this directly to congregations yourself online via their websites in many cases.

- Connecting in understanding

Study the Scriptures to gain understanding of what God's Word says about His plans in these end times. The primary interpretation should be literal but of course the Bible also uses picture language and symbols that are not designed to be taken literally. There are four dimensions in Jewish exegesis of Scripture, known by the acronym 'Pardes' – 1. Peshat - the simple, literal, contextual meaning 2. Remes – the allegoric or symbolic or hinted meaning 3. Derash – the metaphorical sense where the meaning is unfolded through similar passages 4. Sod – esoteric, hidden or mystical meaning.

It is not recommended to search out rabbinic teachings (except Messianic rabbis or Arab Christians) but to ask the Holy Spirit to guide us in reading the Bible as literally as possible. There is much to be gained from a Jewish-Middle Eastern understanding of Scripture unfolded by Messianic teachers as our Western understanding is usually very Greek and humanistically influenced. Jesus was a Jew and still is a Jew and He will not change His ethnicity. He is to be our Bridegroom, so understanding His mindset, culture and His kingdom framework is very helpful.

Bridges for Peace (https://www.bridgesforpeace.com) and Christians4Israel (free bimonthly newspaper - https://www.c4israel.org) provide good teaching material.

- Connecting physically

i. Travel. Tourism in Israel is booming, especially Christian tourism. Travel

November

to and within Israel is not cheap, but if you can afford it, go to Israel and see for yourself the Land of the Bible and the places where Jesus lived, taught, healed, died, rose again and will return. It is guaranteed to change your life and your understanding of Scripture. There are tour groups providing opportunities to go, especially around September and October. However, be selective – choose a tour that does connect with the people; don't just be a tourist. Many tour companies just visit traditional Christian 'holy places', and on these tours you will see lots of old churches, icons, bells and smells but they do not meet the 'living stones'. On other tours, you will meet Jewish Israel, but not Messianic believers. On some others (often the cheaper ones), you will meet Palestinians and be fed Palestinian political propaganda. Again, the *Jewish and Israel Prayer Focus* runs tours focused on prayer and meeting the believers. Prayer for Israel also takes tours, as do most of the large Christian organisations working in Israel.

ii. Serve. If you have time to stay a while, there are many ministries and congregations that welcome volunteers. You will normally be issued a three-month visitors' visa on arrival. This can sometimes be extended to six months but normally you will need to leave the country and then return again if staying longer. Contact the ministry directly to organise this.

iii. If you can't go to Israel, why not have Israel come to you? If you have a spare room, you can host Israeli travellers in your home. Check it out at https://www.celebratemessiah.com.au or email zularoo.hosting@gmail.com.

Prayer Houses and Conferences in Israel

- Elohim House of Prayer – Glenn and Coralie Rowbotham, Mt Carmel 2017, 2018 https://elohimhouse.org
- Intercessors for the Restoration of Israel (Haifa) – David and Josie Silver, Haifa 2004, 2011, 2015 http://www.out-of-zion.com
- City of David Prayer House – connected to Succat Hallel
- Succat Hallel – 24/7 worship ministry – Rick and Patricia Ridings, Jerusalem 2018 https://succathallel.com
- Intercessors for Israel – Intercessory ministry – Chuck Cohen, Ofer Amitai, Jerusalem 2015 https://www.ifi.org.il
- In the Cleft of the Rock – prophetic prayer and teaching – Kathleen Mitchell 2017
- Jerusalem House of Prayer for all Nations – Tom Hess, Jerusalem (Bethphage) jhopfan@jhopfan.org, ancj@jhopfan.org 2015 https://jhopfan.org
- For Zion's Sake Intercessors – 2004
- Jerusalem Prayer Tower – connected to King of Kings Community, Jerusalem – John Ott 2015 http://www.jerusalemprayertower.org
- Prayer House – Dan and Dalia Alon, Mitzpe Ramon 2009, 2017

There are also prayer houses from other nations that conduct meetings in their languages – German, Korean.

Conferences

- Intercessors for Israel conference – January https://www.ifi.org.il
- All Nations Convocation, Jerusalem (Tom Hess' Prayer conference) – September (during the 10 Days of Awe) https://jhopfan.org, ancj@jhopfan.org
- International Christian Embassy Jerusalem conference – October (during the Feast of Tabernacles) https://int.icej.org
- Mt Carmel Assembly runs an annual School of Ministry and Tour https://www.carmelcongregation.org.il/, http://mountcarmelsom.com

November

November Prayer Points: Life from the Dead – Romans chapter 11

1. Rom 11:1-2 Pray for the church to realise that God has not rejected His people.
2. v 3-5 Pray for the faithful remnant of Israel to stay strong and stand up.
3. v 6 Pray for the gospel of God's grace to be preached to those trying to achieve righteousness through the law.
4. v 7-10 Pray for Israel to see that the old way does not work and to seek another way through Yeshua.
5. v 11 Pray for the Gentiles to be thankful that the gospel has come to us because of Israel's transgression and to make our gratitude visible to the Jews.
6. v 12 Pray for the church to grasp that the fullness of the Jews coming to salvation will bring even greater riches (revival) for the church.
7. v 13-14 Pray for the Gentiles to recognise and fulfil their responsibility to make the Jews jealous that they may be saved.
8. v 15 Pray for the church to align itself to God's Word that Israel will be accepted again thus bringing resurrection life.
9. v 16 Pray for Israel to again reflect God's holiness instead of trying to copy the nations.
10. v 17 Pray for the church to understand that we are grafted into the olive tree of Israel partaking with them from the root of Yeshua.
11. v 18 Repent for the church's arrogance against Israel that Paul warns us against.
12. v 19-20 Let us remember that we only remain part of the olive tree by faith, not because we deserve God's favour.
13. v 20-21 Tremble at the thought that we could also be cut off for unbelief.
14. v 22 Pray for the church to remain in and reflect God's kindness.
15. v 23-24 Pray for Israel to come to belief so God can graft them back in again.
16. v 25 Pray for the church to be teachable, not wise in its own human eyes, regarding the Lord's plans to return Israel to the land and Himself. Praise God for His promise that the hardening of the Jew's hearts is only partial and will be reversed.

All Israel Shall be Saved

17. v 25 Pray for the fullness of the Gentiles to come in and for the church and Israel to recognise the last days we live in – that 1948 (rebirth of Israel) and 1967 (return of Jerusalem) were critical events in God's timetable.
18. v 26-27 Remind the Lord of His promise that He will take Israel's sin away, and that all Israel will be saved. Pray that He will hasten that day.
19. v 28 Thank the Lord that the gospel came to us as a result of Israel becoming His enemies for a time, but that His love for Israel has never and will never fail.
20. v 29 Praise God that the gifts and calling of God (for Israel and us) are irrevocable.
21. v 30-32 Praise God for His amazing plan to show mercy to both Jew and Gentile in our disobedience. Thank Him that His mercy triumphs over judgement (James 2:13).
22. v 33-36 Join Paul in his great prayer of thanksgiving to God for the depth of the riches of the wisdom and knowledge of God that is so unfathomable and His awesome plan of redemption for Jew and Gentile alike.
23. Pray for those like Naomi, who have come to Israel after knowing bitterness and tragedy in life, to find the God of Israel and be able to trust in His goodness. Ruth 1:1-6, 20-21
24. Ruth was faithful to Naomi even when it meant leaving behind her family, customs and land. Pray for those that come to Israel to be willing to leave their foreign gods behind and embrace the God of Israel. Ruth 1:16-17
25. Pray for a Gentile Ruth church that will embrace Israel with the love of God, truly grafted in as One New Man. Your people shall be my people and your God my God. Ruth 1:16-17
26. The town of Bethlehem welcomed back their long-lost sister. May Israel also welcome those returning to their homeland and make space for them. Ruth 1:19
27. God's favour and protection were over Ruth because of her diligence and right attitude. Pray for the Ruth church to serve God's people humbly and find provision under His wings. Ruth 2:7-13, 3:11

November

28. Ruth shared what she had gathered. Pray for the rich in Israel to share generously with those who do not have enough and for the Ruth church to do the same. Ruth 2:18
29. Naomi and Boaz knew the law of the kinsman redeemer, and at the appropriate time, Naomi led Ruth to invoke this law for her family. Boaz was a man of integrity and did not impose His will but trusted God. May all godly parents know God's laws and lead their children to walk in them. Ruth 3:1-5, 12-13, 4:1-12
30. Praise the God of restoration. God rewarded Naomi and Ruth and provided for the restoration of their inheritance, children, and even made the Gentile, Ruth, the great-grandmother of King David and part of the royal line of Messiah! Ruth 4:13-22

December

A House of Prayer for all Nations

Photo courtesy Lawrence Hirsch

My house shall be called a house of prayer for all the nations. Is 56:7, Mk 11:17

You also, as living stones, are being built up as a spiritual house for a holy priesthood, to offer up spiritual sacrifices acceptable to God through Jesus Christ...But you are a chosen race, a royal priesthood, a holy nation, a people for God's own possession, so that you may proclaim the excellencies of Him who has called you out of darkness into His marvellous light. I Peter 2:5, 9 (ref Ex 19:5-6)

And many peoples and powerful nations will come to Jerusalem to seek the LORD Almighty and to entreat him. This is what the LORD Almighty says: 'In those days ten people from all languages and nations will take firm hold of one Jew by the hem of his robe and say, "Let us go with you, because we have heard that God is with you."' Zech 8:22-23

December

As we near the end of the year, we will zoom the camera out to see the bigger picture for the nations and also look at the festival of Hanukka which occurs generally in December and occasionally in late November.

One Israeli Jewish believer has a refreshing view of Israel's call to go to the nations today.

Restoring Mission from Israel to the Nations – Gavriel Gefen 2005

We live in a day when the Lord is restoring the nation of Israel. He is restoring the Jewish people physically to the Land of Israel, and He is restoring us spiritually to Himself. This restoration is not an end in itself, but for a purpose. Our God is restoring our nation that we might be restored to our callings.

When I was growing up, my family were hippies in northern California. Then, in 1973, we accepted Yeshua as the Messiah. In 1983, when I was seventeen, my family immigrated back to Israel.

I knew as a teenager that there was a calling on my life to serve the Lord full-time and to go to many nations. Yet, as a new immigrant to Israel, I recognised that missions *from* Israel *to* the nations had not yet been reborn. Many Messianic Jews were travelling out in ministry from Israel to the nations, but two basic dynamics were missing. First of all, few people were ever really sent. There was no sending process, and there was a lack of relational accountability. Secondly, those who were going out were going not so much to be a blessing, but to seek blessing. They were going almost exclusively with the purpose of convincing the nations to bless us – to bless Israel, to bless the Jewish people, to bring the Jews back to Israel, to evangelise the Jews and to give money to Israel, the Messianic Jews, etc. Our congregations were not being given a heart and vision for the nations.

In 1999, a group of Israeli congregational and ministry leaders came together and we founded Keren HaShlichut, an Israeli association of Messianic Jewish emissaries – in other words, an Israeli mission agency. We facilitate the congregational sending of emissaries from Israel to the nations. This has included going to dozens of countries, reaching out to numerous indigenous tribal groups around the world, bringing the Good News to Muslim nations, and active involvement in tsunami relief. We have also begun an initiative to train and send Israelis to work in Bible translation, especially the Hebrew Scriptures.

The Lord is restoring Israel as a nation. He is blessing us, that we might bless others. He is once again blessing the nations through us.

Gavriel Gefen is the founding director of Keren HaShlichut, an Israeli association of Jewish emissaries of Jesus. Gavriel has ministered in over 160 countries of the world.

Judgement Day

God has not only an individual judgement day for us but also a day when the nations will face Him. This is mirrored in the Day of Atonement, when the whole nation was to come before Him in repentance for its sin. The blood of the lamb at Passover delivered the Hebrews from slavery in Egypt and now the blood of the Lamb that has been slain for our sin will deliver us and our nations if it is applied and proven through our actions.

In Matthew 25:31-46 Jesus talks about the judgement of nations (see v 32). He says that the nations will be divided into sheep nations and goat nations. Sheep nations care about the poor and in assisting them, they are ministering to Him also. Goat nations face eternal punishment for their neglect of the 'least of these'. However, the Scripture actually says 'the least of these brothers of Mine' (v 40). The Greek word 'adelphos' actually means 'from the womb'. This aligns with the Old Testament, where Gentile nations were judged when they came against God's people while the Israelites were judged according to how they treated their poor. The church, being grafted in to Israel, will be judged on both accounts. This needs great repentance

December

because the church as a whole has completely missed this understanding and has grossly mistreated Israel through the ages.

Judgement of the Nations – based on article by Chuck Cohen (2015)

Portions of this page came from Why God Judges Nations *by Chuck and Karen Cohen. Their complete article can be read here: http://www.ifi.org.il/teachings. Chuck is a leader of Intercessors for Israel and has an international teaching ministry.*

During the Days of Awe, the Jewish people reflect on God as their King and Judge. This is a time of individual repentance and accountability before our heavenly Father and our fellow man. The Day of Atonement, however, is a day of national repentance. Matt 25:32 mentions the judgement of nations, not individuals. On what basis does God judge nations?

God used Israel in the Old Testament as an example of how He deals with national sin, especially when a nation based upon His laws rebels against Him. Praying for our nations regarding unrighteousness is good, but this may be the symptom rather than the cause of judgement. One result of judgement is that God removes His hand of protection, allowing society to implode. *God gave them up to uncleanness through the lusts of their hearts* (Rom 1:24) and *God gave them over to a reprobate mind, to do the things not right* (Rom 1:26). *Because they did not receive the love of the truth... God shall send them strong delusion that they should believe a lie...*(2 Thess 2:11-12). These are signs that God's restraining grace has been lifted.

What then is the cause? God judges nations according to their leaders' attitudes and actions regarding Israel. Dozens of Scriptures identify this as the root issue. Ezekiel chapters 25-28 is a parade of nations all judged specifically for what they did to Israel. Is 49:24-26, Jer 30:16, 50:10-15, 51:24, Ezek 29:6-7, Zech 1:14-15 are a few of many further examples. Israel's end-time national restoration brings this once again front and centre. The church is meant to be a nation's protection against God's righteous judgement as it stands in intercession for the nation and teaches truth. However, replacement theology, which claims that the church has replaced Israel as God's people, has invaded many churches. This implies that God, who made eternal covenants with Israel, is fickle, forgetful or a liar.

Although God uses nations to judge Israel for her sin, they will also be held accountable for how they treat her. Joel 3:1-2 says that when the Jews are re-gathered to their land, the nations will come to the valley of Jehoshaphat (meaning judgement). The judgement is made because they *scattered My people amongst the nations and divided up My [God's] land.* Matt 25:40 says *to the extent that you did it to one of these brothers of Mine…you did it to me.* Yeshua's brothers are the Jewish people since no church yet existed. God's promise of Genesis 12:3 remains – to bless those who bless Israel and curse those who lightly esteem/despise her.

Wedding Day – The Marriage Supper of the Lamb

The book of Revelation finishes not with judgement but with victory, the wedding of the Lamb and the beginning of a new era of righteousness upon the earth. The later chapters of Isaiah see Israel restored, shining in the glory of the Lord and the nations being drawn to her.

For Zion's sake I will not keep silent, for Jerusalem's sake I will not remain quiet, till her vindication shines out like the dawn, her salvation like a blazing torch. The nations will see your vindication, and all kings your glory; you will be called by a new name that the mouth of the LORD will bestow. You will be a crown of splendor in the LORD's hand, a royal diadem in the hand of your God. No longer will they call you Deserted, or name your land Desolate. But you will be called Hephzibah, and your land Beulah; for the LORD will take delight in you, and your land will be married. As a young man marries a young woman, so will your Builder

December

marry you; as a bridegroom rejoices over his bride, so will your God rejoice over you. Is 62:1-5 (NIV)

It is the intercessors that cry night and day for this to come about - and that is our calling.

I have posted watchmen on your walls, Jerusalem; they will never be silent day or night. You who call on the LORD, give yourselves no rest, and give him no rest till he establishes Jerusalem and makes her the praise of the earth... Pass through, pass through the gates! Prepare the way for the people. Build up, build up the highway! Remove the stones. Raise a banner for the nations. Is 62:6-7,10 (NIV)

We are not only to pray but also to declare to Israel the Lord's proclamation of her destiny:

The LORD has made proclamation to the ends of the earth: "Say to Daughter Zion, 'See, your Savior comes! See, his reward is with him, and his recompense accompanies him.'" They will be called the Holy People, the Redeemed of the LORD; and you will be called Sought after, the City no longer deserted. Is 62:11-12 (NIV)

As we do this, we are preparing the way for the return of Yeshua as King over the nations, ruling in righteousness over His rightful inheritance. We are also preparing Israel to receive her Saviour and take her place as the bride ruling with Him as one with the called out *ekklesia* of God, serving Him as a kingdom of priests and a holy nation (Ex 19:6). We pray for the day when both the church and Israel, as His bride, are washed clean and clothed in white, with our lamps lit, ready for His arrival.

All Israel Shall be Saved

Hallelujah! For our Lord God Almighty reigns. Let us rejoice and be glad and give him glory! For the wedding of the Lamb has come and his bride has made herself ready. Fine linen, bright and clean, was given her to wear. (Fine linen stands for the righteous acts of God's holy people.) Then the angel said to me, "Write this: Blessed are those who are invited to the wedding supper of the Lamb!" And he added, "These are the true words of God." Rev 19:7-9

Hanukka – Re-dedicating God's Temple

Hanukka (the Feast of Dedication) commemorates the battle of the sons of Zion over the sons of Greece which precedes the coming of the Lord (Zech 9:13-16).

For I will bend Judah as My bow, I will fill the bow with Ephraim. And I will stir up your sons, O Zion, against your sons, O Greece; and I will make you like a warrior's sword. Then the LORD will appear over them, and His arrow will go forth like lightning; and the Lord GOD will blow the trumpet, and will march in the storm winds of the south. Zech 9:13-14

The prophet Daniel had visions of the kingdoms of Babylon, Medo-Persia, Greece and Rome that led up to the coming of the Messiah. The Hebrew Masoretic text and protestant Bible do not include the inter-testamental books, which are included in the Greek Septuagint translation of the Hebrew. Catholic Bibles do include these apocryphal books, four of which are the historical books of Maccabees. These cover the 'silent' four hundred years of history before the birth of Jesus.

During the years 330-149 BCE, after Alexander the Great conquered vast territory, Greek culture was imposed on the subjects, including the worship of their multitude of gods. Hellenisation crept into Hebrew society and corruption into the priesthood. The High Priesthood was sold to the highest bidder and immorality and pagan rituals were practised in the Temple precincts.

December

In 171 BCE, Antiochus IV Epiphanes (meaning 'god manifest') came to power. He directed the Jews to 'forbid burnt offerings and sacrifices and drink offerings in the sanctuary, to profane Sabbaths and feasts, to defile the sanctuary and the priests, to build altars and sacred precincts and shrines for idols, to sacrifice swine and other unclean animals, and to leave their sons uncircumcised' (1 Macc 1:45-48). Whoever would not obey his orders was to be put to death. At the first resistance, he reacted with venom, erecting a 'desolating sacrifice' on the altar of the Lord in the Temple (Dan 8:11-12, 11:31, Mk 13:14), by sacrificing a pig in the Temple thus desecrating the altar of the Lord, and pouring its blood in the Holy of Holies and its broth on the scrolls before cutting them to pieces! This occurred on the birthday celebration of Zeus (25 December, 25th day of Kislev, the winter solstice – dawn of the new sun). He began to demand worship, setting up a statue of Zeus in the temple (with his face on it!) and ordered people to bow down to it. His vicious actions fulfilled Daniel 9:27, as 'one who makes desolate' in the Temple of God. Jesus referred to this verse in Matt 24:15 when He talked of a future anti-Christ to come.

Some courageous Jews began to fight for the restoration of God's laws and His temple. One brave man, Mattathias, drew the line and refused to obey even if it meant his life. He began a revolt and his son Judas Maccabees (hammer head) continued in his wake. Many lost their lives but eventually the Jewish forces managed to drive out the Greeks and re-dedicate the Temple. The festival of Hanukka (dedication), on the 25th day of the month of Kislev, remembers this event. Jesus was in the Temple for this festival.

At that time the Feast of the Dedication took place at Jerusalem; it was winter and Jesus was walking in the temple in the portico of Solomon. The Jews gathered around Him and were saying to Him, 'How long will you keep us in suspense? If you are the Messiah, tell us plainly.' Jesus answered them, 'I told you and you do not believe...because you are not of my sheep. My sheep hear my voice...I and the Father are one.' The Jews took up stones...to stone Him (for blasphemy). John 10:22-33

'The one who makes desolate' is a pattern for the anti-Christ figure who wants to destroy God's people and set himself up on the throne of God. We are in the same battleground today. Greek-based secular humanism is the accepted 'religion' of our day, which is taught as truth which may not to be questioned. Greek thinking has invaded our schools, society and the church also, in the form of humanism (the Greeks worshiped gods in the form of humans, not animals like their predecessors), demanding allegiance to the modern gods of evolution, multiculturalism, the homosexual agenda, climate change, and including embracing death itself through abortion and euthanasia.

We need some modern Judas Maccabees who have the courage to take a stand for God and His righteousness. This is not a physical fight (though one may physically suffer), but a battle for our minds and hearts. A luke-warm church is only worthy of being spat out of the Lord's mouth (Rev 3:15-16). If we are not upsetting the secular *status quo* of our society, we know we are luke-warm. The question which confronted Jesus in the Temple during this festival was His deity – *If you are the Messiah, tell us plainly* (John 10:24). He did and they picked up stones to kill him. Today it is no different. There is no fuss when we say that Jesus did many good works or even proclaim Him a teacher or prophet, as Islam does. However, when we proclaim Him as the Son of God and the only Messiah, the world begins to pick up stones to stone us too. Hanukka is our example to take a stand for Jesus and for truth.

Tradition of the Multiplication of the Oil

According to Talmudic tradition (Shabbat 21b), when the Greeks were evicted, the priests only found enough ritually pure consecrated oil to light the Menorah for one day and it took seven days to consecrate the holy oil (Ex 29:37). The priests lit the candelabra anyway, and God multiplied the oil until the new batch was ready and the lamp in the temple continued to burn miraculously for eight days until the fresh oil was ready. To commemorate this, the nine-branched menorah (Hanukkia) is lit at Hanukka. One candle is lit the first day from the 'servant' candle, and an extra one each day until all eight plus the 'servant' candle are lit. All candles are to be lit from the servant candle. The menorah must be set in the window of the house for all to see. This is a beautiful picture of Jesus, the light of the world, who gives us the holy oil to allow us to shine His light and set us on a lampstand so we can be the light to the dark world.

Let your light shine before men that they may see your good works and glorify your Father who is in heaven. Matt 5:16

As we approach the end of this time together for the year, we have a timely reminder that darkness cannot overpower the light.

In the beginning was the Word, and the Word was with God, and the Word was God...In Him was life; and the life was the light of men. And the light shines in the darkness; and the darkness did not overpower it. Jn 1:1,4-5

December Prayer Points – Hanukka and the Nations

1. Hanukka 1st night – At this Feast of the Re-dedication of the temple, also known as the Festival of Lights, pray for Israel to see the Light. Is 9:2
2. Hanukka 2nd night. Hanukka is the victory of the Maccabees over the Greeks. May God raise up valiant, prudent warriors like David, to lead the army in times of war. 1 Sam 16:18
3. Hanukka 3rd night. During WWI, it was during Hanukka in 1917 that the ANZACs entered Jerusalem and the city was handed over to the British and Allied forces. May Israel know that it is God who gives the victory. Ps 20:7

All Israel Shall be Saved

4. Hanukka 4th night. May Israel seek the good shepherd and know His voice. Jn 10:26-27
5. Hanukka 5th Night. May there be a revelation to many that I and the Father are one. Jn 10:30
6. Hanukka 6th Night. Pray for the believers in the Land to do the works of the Father as Jesus did so they will shine as a light to the nation. Jn 10:32
7. Hanukka 7th night. Pray for many like Judas Maccabee and his family to arise and lead the nation in defending righteousness even if it costs them their lives. Phil 1:21
8. Hanukka 8th night. Pray for many to hear the call that Jesus is the Son of God and call Him Lord. As C. S. Lewis said, 'He must be a Liar, a Lunatic or the Lord.' Jn 10:36
9. Pray for God to raise up an army of evangelists from amongst the Messianic Jewish believers with a vision for the nations. Rev 7:4-7
10. Pray for God to turn the hearts of the Israeli pastors and teachers going to the nations from seeking blessing for Israel to seeking to bless the nations. Gen 12:2-3
11. Pray for Jewish followers of Jesus taking His message to the nations. Lk 10:2-12
12. Pray for those communicating Jesus to have wisdom and not impede the message by imposing unnecessary hindrances and barriers to Jesus. Acts 15:19-20
13. Pray for each people, nation, tongue and tribe to discover for itself what it means to be faithful to Jesus within their own heritage. Gal 5:1
14. Praise God for those who are going out from Israel with the gospel and with humanitarian aid to help the poorer nations. Acts 8:14-17
15. Pray for wisdom and anointing for those being sent. Acts 13:1-4
16. Pray for a maturing of the Israeli congregations to recognise the need to send missionaries to the nations. Is 42:6-8, 49:6
17. As Gavriel is mainly visiting first-nations people groups, pray that they will understand the gospel in their own cultural way, not adopt a 'Western' Jesus. Phil 1:27-30
18. Pray for the first-nations people groups to connect with Israel and God's global purposes. Ps 33:12

December

19. Pray for the church to understand that they will face end-time judgement based on how they treat Israel as God's representative. Joel 3:1-3
20. Pray for your nation to be a sheep nation. Matt 25:31-33,40
21. Pray for Jews and Christians to come into their prophetic destiny as God's witnesses and the light/menorah of the world. Matt 5:14-16, Acts 1:8
22. May the Christian pilgrims visiting Israel at Christmas time be a light to the Jews. Rom 10:19
23. Pray for protection over the land from all attacks during the Christmas celebrations. Ps 91:1-7
24. May the Glory of the Lord appear over His people and nations and kings come to the brightness of Israel's rising. Is 60:1-3
25. On this Christmas Day, may the people walking in darkness see a great Light and recognise the Messiah (Is 42:16). Pray for revelation of Messiah for the Jewish people. Acts 2:17
26. Pray for the wealth of nations be brought to Israel. Is 60:5-6,11
27. May the sons of Israel be willing to return to the land with their wealth and the ships of Tarshish be ready to bring them home. Is 60:9
28. Pray for the foreigners in the nations to build up the walls of Jerusalem. Is 60:10
29. Pray for foreign nations to understand that they dishonour God's people at their own peril. Is 60:12
30. Pray for the Messianic and Arab believers to walk as children of light in all goodness and righteousness and truth. Eph 5:8-9
31. May Israel recognise that Yeshua is the Light of the World and prepare herself to be the bride of Christ. Jn 8:12, Rev 19:7-9

Appendix 1: Relating to Jewish People

Witnessing to Jews - Lawrence Hirsch 2004

Most people don't realise that the Gospel was good news to Jews before it became good news for Gentiles. People tend to forget that Jesus was Jewish and that all his early followers and the writers of the New Testament were all Jewish. Faith in Jesus is faith in the Jewish Messiah. This is a foundational principle to remember when witnessing to your Jewish friend.

Practical Tips

- *Be a friend.* Let your friendship and love be genuine irrespective of your friend's response to the Gospel.
- *Be a credible witness* to the life-changing reality of the Messiah's presence in your life. Remember your life speaks more than your words.
- *Watch your language.* Certain words may have totally different, even offensive, meanings to your Jewish friend. Often, such words as 'cross' and 'Christ' bring up collective memories of persecution by so-called 'Christians.' Be sensitive.
- *Present a person.* Try to direct your conversation with your Jewish friend to the person of Jesus, rather than speaking about religion and denominations.
- *Offer your priestly ministry.* Jewish people may reject your prophetic ministry of proclaiming the Gospel, but they seldom reject your priestly ministry of prayer. Find out how you can pray for your Jewish friend and offer to pray for them immediately, or later in your own time.
- *Share your testimony.* Jewish people are often fascinated by your testimony.
- *Affirm Jewish identity.* Because we are brought up believing that we cannot be Jewish and believe in Jesus, it is important that you regularly affirm your friend's Jewish identity and remind them that they do not have to give up being Jewish to believe in the Jewish Messiah.
- *Ask questions.* The very best way to learn is to ask questions.
- *Invite your Jewish friend to your church or to a Messianic congregation.* Once you've been witnessing to your Jewish friend, it would be good to

introduce them to another Messianic Jew. However, if you're a Gentile believer don't underestimate the important role God has for you in witnessing to your Jewish friend. Remember what Paul said: ... *because of their transgression, salvation has come to the Gentiles to make Israel envious.* Rom 11:11

Celebrate Messiah's desire is to be a resource to the church and to Christians in their witnessing to Jewish people. We have wonderful materials that will help you in this endeavour and will also help you understand better the Jewish roots of the Christian faith.
https://www.celebratemessiah.com.au
Phone: 61 3 9563 5544

In the US, you can contact Chosen People Ministries   https://www.chosenpeople.com Email info@chosenpeople.com Telephone 212.223.2252 Toll-free: 888.293.7482

Barriers to be Removed by Prayer – Jill Curry 2002, 2006, updated 2020

It is said that where there are two Jews, there are three opinions. In the yeshivot (Jewish Bible colleges), lively debate is par for the course and they generally seem to be able to encompass differing theological points of view, easier than Christians – except when it comes to the acceptance of Messianic believers as part of Judaism. This is especially the case with certain groups of the ultra-orthodox community who campaign vigorously against the Jewish believers in Jesus/Yeshua. While this is an extreme view, not held by many, most Jews have many obstacles to faith in Jesus as the Jewish Messiah. Below are a few of the difficulties they may have to work through. Pray for these stones to be removed (Is 62:10-12).

Spiritual Barriers

- The Scriptures say that God has blinded the eyes of the Jewish people for a time (Rom 11:25). Pray for the veil to be removed (2 Cor 3:14-16).
- Hardness of heart (Ezek 3:7). Pray for the stubbornness to be melted (Ezek 36:26).
- Israel today is crying out to be a prosperous, secular, humanistic nation like other western nations instead of a nation set apart for God (1 Sam chapter 8, 12:12-17).
- Many religious Jews are seeking God through Kabbalah – religious mysticism that has many occult elements and unbiblical teachings (Matt 24:11).
- Wealth (Matt 19:23-26)

Emotional Barriers

Throughout the ages, Christian history has an appalling record of anti-Semitism, hatred and murder against the Jews. Jews associate the Cross more readily with forced conversions and pogroms rather than a symbol of love. This negative image is slowly changing as many Christian organisations are helping the Jews return from the diaspora, giving them loving practical assistance in the land, coming to the land and supporting them.

Intellectual Barriers

- Many Jews do not have a good knowledge of their Scriptures, just as is the case with many Christians. Even in yeshivot (Bible Colleges) the teachings of the rabbis often take precedence over the teaching of the Word of God (2 Tim 3:1-17).
- The problem for the disciples in Jesus' day was that their expectation of the 'Kingdom of Heaven' was political, not in their hearts (Acts 1:3, 6-8). Nothing has changed. Many look at this broken world and conclude that the Messiah has not yet come (Lk 17:20-21).
- I know a number of Jews who have experienced the love of Christians and feel that Jesus is the Messiah for the Gentiles, who is restoring the

Christians back to their roots, but they still await a Messiah who is King of the Jews (Jn 19:19-22).

Theological Barriers

- Probably the greatest theological difficulty for Jews is to believe in the divinity of Jesus as God. Most Jewish thought depicts the Messiah as a human person who is anointed with power from God, but not God Himself embodied in human form (Jn 1:1-18).
- Associated with this is the concept of the Trinity. This is even a problem for some Messianic believers. Judaism has no difficulty with the concept of the Ruach HaKodesh (Holy Spirit) but the Son of God with Jesus being equal and a part of the Godhead is quite another matter. Although He never overtly called Himself God, He did receive worship and in numerous other terms claimed to be the fulfilment of the Old Testament prophecies of the Messiah. This is blasphemy if He is not God – and for this He was nailed to the cross. Without the resurrection, these people could have been right (1 Cor 15:16-22).
- Isaiah chapter 53 is explained in various ways, but normally Jews say it refers to Israel as the suffering servant. Verses 4-5 differentiate between 'He' who bore 'our' sins. 'He' and 'our' cannot be the same person. One cannot be a substitute for oneself. Besides, the Torah is quite clear that the only sacrifice for sin was the life in the blood of an animal (Lev 17:11). The suffering and death of the Messiah is indeed very un-king-like, but that is what the Father did for us (Jn 3:16). The Cross is still a stumbling block (1 Cor 1:22-25).
- Some Jews believe that it is a repentant heart that God sees and forgives, so we do not need Jesus to intercede for us. If that were the case, why was the whole sacrificial system instituted? Not to mention the annual dramatic enactment on the Day of Atonement for the sins of the nation. Even the High Priest could not enter into God's presence without first making a sacrifice for himself (Lev 16:11). Our righteousness is as filthy rags (Is 64:6). Praise God for the blood of Jesus which cleanses us from all unrighteousness (1 Jn 1:5-10). Our sacrifice is now our service and worship to God (Rom 12:1-2).

Appendix 1

Social Barriers

Many believers are ostracised from their families and rejected by their friends and community when they accept Jesus. Some have lost jobs, been divorced by their husbands or wives or lost their visas. For many, their identity as a Jew is at stake. This is nothing new but is a high price to pay. The support of a new family (the church) and discipleship in a new identity in Him (2 Cor 5:17) is crucial.

Physical Barriers

Few Jews even know a Jewish believer in Jesus and some believers do not have the courage to make their faith known publicly for fear of persecution. More workers are needed in the harvest field Matt (9:37-38). How can they hear without a preacher (Rom 10:14)? Pray for boldness (2 Tim 1:7).

Most Jews have been taught in school the stories from the Old Testament, but they have little knowledge of who God really is and have not been led into a living relationship with Him. Jesus is mentioned once in passing in the Israeli history curriculum in a brief chapter covering the Greco-Roman period. A survey of ninth-grade school students carried out a week before Christmas in 1999 revealed that most students did not know even basic details, such as where Jesus was born, lived or died, when He lived or even that He was a Jewish rabbi *(Ha'Aretz newspaper, 23 Dec, 1999)*.

What Israeli Jews do know, however, is the long history of persecution of the Jewish people by the Christians, of which most of the church is unaware. They know that the Jews fled out of Spain when the Christian leaders forced them to convert or die. They know that the conquest of the Crusaders meant death for the Jews. Many early settlers to Israel came as refugees from the pogroms in the late 19th and early 20th centuries in Eastern Europe and Russia. They were often accused of being 'Christkillers' and Christian holidays were used as excuses for pogroms. Most Jews think that the Holocaust was caused by Christians, because Germany was officially a Christian country.

All Israel Shall be Saved

For these historical reasons and some theological problems, Jews (especially the orthodox) have rejected Christianity and are often very hostile at any broaching of the subject. Many believe that Christians worship another God (or even three gods). Jesus is commonly referred to as 'Yeshu', rather than the biblical 'Yeshua'. The first is an acronym standing for 'may his name be blotted out'. The second means 'one who saves'.

It is only the power of prayer, the sovereign work of the Holy Spirit and a demonstration of love that will leap these barriers, but the following hints may be helpful.

- Let your Jewish friends know that the Lord loves them with an everlasting love (Is 43:1-4, 49:14-16, Jer 31:3-4) and He has never and will never forsake them. Show them the prophetic Scriptures about God's promises to return them to the land of their forefathers and the Lord's purposes of pouring His Spirit upon them (eg Ezek 36:26-28, Jer 31:31-34).
- Do not argue with Jews about their concept of history. Stand in the gap, confess the church's errors and ask forgiveness for our wrongdoings.
- Ask them if they have ever had a dream or vision where a man in white appeared to them. Jesus is visiting many Jews and Muslims in this way. If they have, ask them about the dream or vision and what they understood by it. Also ask if they have had a miraculous experience in their life where God seemed to have intervened.
- Preach the gospel from the Old Testament (especially Messianic prophecies such as Isaiah chapter 53) as Jesus and Paul did (Lk 24:27). Use the books of Matthew and Hebrews, which orthodox Jews will easily identify as Jewish. Point out that Jesus was and is a Jew, all the first disciples were Jewish and most of the writers of the New Testament were Jewish. Show how Jesus fulfilled the Feasts and became the Passover Lamb and the Great High Priest.
- Use terminology they will understand better, such as 'Yeshua' rather than 'Jesus' and 'kehilah' rather than 'church'.
- Tell them they need to follow Yeshua, rather than 'convert to Christianity'. (Conversion means persecution in their minds). Let them know that there are thousands of Jewish believers in the world today, and about 80

Appendix 1

congregations in Israel.
- Show hospitality. Israelis love to travel. Celebrate Messiah now has a hosting service called 'Zularoo'. You can host travelling Israelis in your home and show them love, friendship and share the gospel as opportunities arise. Contact zularoo.hosting@gmail.com or https://www.celebratemessiah.com.au. New Zealand has similar opportunities.
- Tell them how Jesus changed your life. No one can deny a personal testimony. Talk about your personal relationship with the Lord – how He speaks to you, guides you and rebukes you. It is a revelation to most Jews that God speaks to people today.

Jill Curry founded the Jewish Prayer Focus in 2002 and has coordinated the ministry since then.
http://jewishandisraelprayerfocus.org

Appendix 2: Testimonies

For your encouragement and edification, I have gathered a few of the testimonies that have been presented over the years in the Jewish Prayer Focus. They include a PLO terrorist, a rabbi, a schizophrenic paranoid, a professor of secular atheism, a cave dweller, a drug addict and a violent youth. Jesus has healed and restored them all. Most are now leading congregations or ministries.

The organisation 'One for Israel' is gathering a large collection of testimonies on video and are presenting them on the web, not only in English but also in Hebrew and gathering millions of hits. This is modern evangelism. They also offer teaching on how to become a believer and answer Jewish questions about Messiah. All these are proving popular and a great tool to reach Jews who would never enter a church or even openly be seen questioning such matters. https://www.oneforisrael.org

Testimonies can also be seen on http://www.messianicgoodnews.org

1. A 20th Century Saul – Rabbi Harold Vallins 2002

Rabbi Harold was ordained as a rabbi in 1970 at the Leo Baeck Theological College in London. 'As a Jewish boy, I had been taught to hate Jesus because of the heartache and atrocities brought upon the Jews in His name.' After a lifetime of studying Hebrew, Jewish history, theology and customs and preaching against Jesus, he saw the life of one of his congregation change so dramatically that he set out to investigate the cause.

Brian had been transformed from a hard-hearted businessman after attending a prayer breakfast with a group of business associates. Rabbi Harold was intrigued and began to meet with these men. In February 1998, he went with them to a Presidential Prayer Breakfast in Washington. The next day, as the men shared together and joined in prayer, the rabbi was transported to another plane and 'saw' and 'met' Jesus. The Lord spoke to him by name. 'Harold, I am calling you. I want you to work with me.' He responded, 'Jesus, you are my Messiah, my Lord, my Saviour!'" Harold shook and wept under the Lord's touch. He was bewildered and shocked at what he had just said.

The following day, as he walked through the Holocaust Museum pondering why he had previously been so angry at Jesus, a woman approached him, asked if he was the rabbi from Melbourne and gave him the following Scripture: Jeremiah 1:4-10. *'Before I formed you in your mother's womb I knew you. Before you were born I consecrated you: I appointed you a prophet to the nations…You must go to everyone I send you and say whatever I command you. Do not be afraid of them for I am with you and will rescue you', declares the Lord… 'See today I appoint you over nations and over kingdoms, to uproot and tear down, to destroy and to overthrow, to build and to plant'.*

Harold understood that God was telling him that he had to uproot and tear down his former learning and after that God would build and plant. His life had changed forever.

After returning home, his wife left him, he was asked to resign from his rabbinate and he lost his congregation and his Jewish friends. In his hour of despair, Jesus gathered him in His arms, poured His oil of comfort over him and restored him, so he could rejoice in his sufferings. 'I have reached a deeper level of knowing why I have been "chosen".'

Rabbi Harold passed away in 2009. He was also barred from sharing the gospel with his young son on threat of never seeing him again. He paid a high price for choosing to follow Christ.

----

2. From Caveman to 'Rabbi' - Eitan Shishkoff 2005

Despite growing up in an American family where my parents spared no expense to provide for us, I found myself a disillusioned university dropout, raging against the system, and trying to find utopia in the alternative lifestyle of drugs and rock music.

Appendix 2

After marrying Connie, we moved to New Mexico and lived in a cave. We learned to survive for four years by cooking on wood stoves, hauling buckets of water, using outdoor toilets and lighting with kerosene lanterns. We overcame snakes, drought, disease and personal conflicts. Connie almost died twice in childbirth. We were desperately seeking spiritual reality and searched in Hopi and Pueblo Indian mythology, astrology and Eastern mysticism.

Tragedy struck when my buddy, a young father, was killed by a bullet. He was innocent, and questions about life and death raced through my mind. Two 'Jesus people' provided the answer. They spoke of Yeshua as the Messiah – atoning for the evil of the world. They even pointed to His prophecy of Israel's modern-day restoration. I had thought of Jesus as an ascended master. I rejected the concept of a personal Saviour, much less a Creator. As hip, intellectual Jews seeking for truth, the New Testament 'Jesus' was an alternative we hadn't been ready to consider. But while they spoke, I saw His face of compassion as He was executed for my pride and self-centeredness. When I said 'Yes' to Him, an enormous weight lifted from my shoulders and deep guilt was rolled away.

Others in our commune also began to accept Yeshua and lives were transformed. I wanted to help more people to find this relationship with God and decided to go to Bible College. We were fortunate to find a Messianic Jewish 'father' who mentored us and helped us relate our Jewish life to our new-found faith. After these formative years, we headed east, to Washington DC to be part of a Messianic congregation where our children had their Bar and Bat Mitzvah and I became a Messianic 'rabbi'.

Twenty years after receiving Yeshua (1972-1992), we have made 'aliya' and become part of the miracle of the restoration of God's people to their land. In 1989, God gave me a vivid vision of an oasis, which I understood was God's 'tents of mercy' for Jewish exiles returning to Israel. This refuge provided practical assistance and the spiritual water of Yeshua's healing and atonement (Jer 30:18). This oasis has materialised into five congregations and humanitarian aid centres from Haifa Bay to the Sea of Galilee. We encourage the formation of small businesses and we have opened a textile factory. We also train leaders and reach out to plant congregations in Israel and the nations.

Eitan saw the need for youth in Israel's Messianic congregations to understand their faith as rooted in the Hebrew Scriptures and native to Israel. This led to the creation of *Katzir* (harvest), a ministry that has organized youth conferences for inspiration, instruction and fellowship since 1999. This passion has given rise to a new vision to create an equipping village called *Fields of Wheat* that will train both Jewish and Arab believers as true disciples of Yeshua and workers to gather in the final harvest before His return.

Eitan Shishkoff lives in Haifa, Israel. He and Connie have been married for 51 years. They have four children and eleven grandchildren who all live in Israel. He is the founding director of 'Tents of Mercy' network of congregations and humanitarian aid https://www.tentsofmercy.org; *Katzir National Youth; and* Fields of Wheat: Equipping for Harvest https://www.fieldsofwheat.org.

----

3. Violence to Victory - Pastor Joseph Haddad 2007

In May 2000 the Israeli army withdrew from southern Lebanon and 7,000 southern Lebanese Army soldiers, who were allied with Israeli Defence Forces, had to flee from Hezbollah, leaving behind their homes, properties and loved ones to cross the border into Israel where they were offered refuge. For 25 years, those faithful Lebanese had paid a high price to defend the northern borders of Israel from terrorist organisations. The Carmel Assembly in Haifa responded to their plight. God had prepared Joseph and Ibtissam Haddad, who had been training in Bible College in the 1990s.

Appendix 2

Joseph was born to Lebanese parents, in Haifa, Israel and raised in a nominal Arab Christian family. He attended the Catholic church at Christmas and Easter to meet friends rather than worship the Lord. As a teenager, he embarked on a sinful lifestyle, mistreated his elderly parents both verbally and physically and was living in total despair. In August 1983, his parents brought him a bride from Lebanon. He was happy and thought this would change his life, but from their first week of marriage his inner emptiness caused him to abuse, curse and humiliate her. Only divine intervention prevented her returning to her parents in Lebanon. Joseph was losing hope.

About six months into their marriage, they were visiting relatives in Haifa, when three believing brothers shared the good news with them. For the first time, Joseph heard that Jesus could forgive his sins and start his life anew. The Holy Spirit convicted him immediately and he spontaneously started weeping and repenting and asking God's forgiveness while tears flowed like a river. He hugged and kissed his wife and begged her forgiveness. He ran home, got some water, washed his parents' feet and asked their forgiveness. His father joyfully received him into his loving arms as the prodigal son in Luke chapter 15. Joseph echoed Paul's words, *Jesus Christ came into the world to save sinners, of whom I am the worst* (1 Tim 1:15).

When his parents saw the transformation in his life and despite their old age, they also received Jesus as their Lord and Saviour. His father immediately quit smoking and they loved to sit and have Joseph read the Scriptures to them, as they had poor eyesight. They praised God for changing their son's stony heart into a new loving heart. When unbelieving neighbours came to visit they were astonished that the aggressive youth was now loving and kind to his parents and honouring his wife.

How awesome is God, using a Messianic congregation to train an Arab pastor to lead a Lebanese congregation that reaches out to Jews! The One New Man of Eph 2:14-16 is emerging!

Joseph and Ibtissam's Lebanese congregation on the northern coast of Israel, includes Jews, Arabs, ex-Muslims, and Christians. The youth of the congregation attend Jewish schools, where they witness to their classmates and the neighbourhood friends, and are receiving many requests for Hebrew Bibles including the New Testament! joehadad@inter.net.il River of God Lebanese Congregation in Nahariya, PO Box 9511 Haifa 31094 Israel

----

4. Saved from Atheism – Victor and Julia Blum 2007 (updated 2020)

I, Victor Blum, was born into an atheistic Jewish academic family in Estonia 60 years ago. I graduated from Tartu University (Estonia) with MA degrees in History and Philosophy. While in Tartu, I met my wife Julia at the students' philosophical club and we married in 1984. Julia came from Kiev (Ukraine), escaping unrestrained anti-Semitism there, to study computers. After my graduation, I lectured in Philosophy (including Scientific Atheism) in the same university, with popular acclaim and travelled overseas taking part in scientific forums.

In Soviet-occupied Estonia, any form of Judaism was strictly forbidden, so we had never met a believer. In the summer of 1990, we had an encounter that would change our lives forever. In a beautiful coastal resort, we met a young pastor, who was 'fishing' specifically for Jewish people! A year later, we both received the Messiah, and then in November 1991 God brought us straight to Jerusalem.

Appendix 2

Leaving behind families, friends, and successful scientific careers, without any theological or denominational backgrounds, ties or connections, I came to Jerusalem with the credentials of the first ever diplomat, official representative of the Estonian Republic in the State of Israel.

Towards the end of 1992, we started to minister the gospel to the new immigrants from the former Soviet Union. A few dozen Russian Jewish immigrants came to know the Lord which over the years grew into a Russian-speaking Congregation of 100 people called *Even Yisrael* (Rock of Israel). Many of these believers became mature and they now serve the Lord in different congregations in Israel and overseas. We also ministered as evangelists in Arad and Ashdod and as congregational leaders in Ariel.

I have served on various leadership teams, boards and committees that work in the fields of discipling and teaching biblical Jewish roots, Messianic education, and increasing integrity and unity of the Body of Messiah in the Land. Besides congregational leadership, Julia has written thorough and profound discourses on Biblical texts with deep Hebrew insights that have touched many hearts, and have been translated into several languages.

I joined Chosen People Ministries (CPM) in June 2004, and four years later we moved to New York City for three years of studies and ministry with CPM. In August 2011 we returned home to Jerusalem and started a new ministry. The vision is to reach mostly Russian-speaking Israelis and create a highly integrated, vibrant, home-based congregation or chain of congregations actively serving in and around Jerusalem, modelled after the first Jewish Messianic congregations in the Book of Acts.

I also minister to Holocaust survivors, and am preparing the believers both spiritually and practically for the upcoming new waves of the Jewish emigration to the Land. I help plant and spiritually equip the Messianic congregations in Eastern Europe (Acts 1:8) in close cooperation with local believers. I travel to different countries and first meet there with the Christian leadership. As part of this calling I am working to build a bridge between Messianic and non-Messianic (Christian) congregations. In October

All Israel Shall be Saved

2013, the first ever Messianic conference was held in Tallinn, Estonia.

Julia continues to teach, write and lecture. She is working for Israel Institute of Biblical Studies, and has a weekly blog (blog.israelbiblicalstudies.com) on Jewish Studies and biblical themes. She also teaches Bible online in cooperation with the 'E-teacher Company'. Her books can be found at https://www.amazon.com/Julia-Blum/e/B00LUY0JN8/ref=sr_ntt_srch_lnk_8?qid=1474990243&sr=8-8

Victor and Julia have three children: daughter Yael, 31, and two boys, Daniel (23) who is currently working in hi-tech in Tel Aviv and Yoel (20) who is currently serving in the army.

----

5. A New Creation – Israel Harel 2011

I was born in Israel of parents who had had tough lives and consequently could not meet my emotional needs. As a shy, plump child, my friends ridiculed me and I reacted by becoming rebellious. At 15, I was convinced that music and drugs were the answer to the world's ills. I joined a hippie group, lived on the streets, slept in parks and begged for money. One day, a woman invited us to her home and offered us food. We were glad and stayed for a fortnight. Before meals, she showed us how Yeshua had fulfilled the prophecies about the Messiah and explained that we must be born again. She asked,

'Do you believe?' To avoid being thrown out, we all said 'Yes'! Although interested, I wasn't ready to submit to anyone. Like Jonah, I ran away from God for six years.

Deep in the morass of sin, and despairing of life, I swallowed a lot of non-prescription drugs and was admitted to the psychiatric hospital. Classified as a schizophrenic paranoid, I was treated for over two years with drugs that didn't help. A psychiatric hospital is riddled with demons and there is no peace. I would break windows or attack someone, so that with intravenous Valium I could get a few hours of deep nightmare-free sleep! After attacking a psychologist, I was discharged! I lived alone in the forest, devoid of hope and suicidal. To relieve my boredom, I started reading my Bible again. A ray of light penetrated my dark soul and I found a new inner peace.

On a ferry to Patmos, I found my cabin mates were believers on their way to a Christian Youth Center in Cyprus. I joined them at the camp. As I was prayed for, I saw Messiah with His arms outstretched, saying 'I love you.' I finally broke down and wept. 'Take my life and do with me as you will!' I worked there for a year, being loved, counselled and discipled. One day, I saw myself standing underneath a waterfall of streaming light, which swept over me and washed me from inside out. Again I saw the Messiah and ran towards Him. He picked me up and embraced me. The prodigal had finally come home.

I returned to Israel a new truly-changed person. Now sane and healthy, I visited the psychiatrist who couldn't believe his eyes and kept muttering, 'What a miracle!' I told him that Yeshua saved me from drowning. My relationship with my family has now been renewed and my father, who at first didn't want to talk to me, gave his life to Yeshua just days before he died. One sister is also a believer. Whilst working in Tel-Aviv, I met my Swiss wife, Shlomit. We married in 1982, have three children, and five grandchildren and have served the Lord in full-time ministry leading evangelism, starting new congregations, teaching and writing books, since 1991. www.harelfamily.net

----

6. Palestinian Sniper now Saving Jews – Tass Saada 2013

Taysir (Tass) Saada was born in a tent in a refugee camp in Gaza in 1951 and grew up in Saudi Arabia, where his family was unwelcome in the strict

All Israel Shall be Saved

Islamic culture practised there. The climate of intimidation turned Tass into an angry, resentful, violent child. His family started a car-repair business serving King Saud and later his family immigrated to Qatar. Shortly after the Arab humiliation in the Six Day war in Israel in 1967, Tass decided to run away and join Arafat's forces. His chief motivation was to destroy

Israel and liberate Palestine. At age 17, he was trained as a sniper in the Fatah movement, sent on assignments to kill Jewish leaders and he occasionally acted as a driver for Yasser Arafat. He trained 9-13 year old boys as fighters in Fatah training camps. In his misappropriated zeal and hatred he saw Christian Arabs as spies for Israel and also went after them.

After being coerced back home to Qatar, his bad attitude and violence caused his family so much grief that they agreed for him to travel to the US. In order to get permanent residency, he married an American. He became a workaholic in the restaurant/hotel business, hardly seeing his children and blowing much money on women and nightclubs.

At a desperate time in his life, his friend Charlie Sharpe told him of a Jew who was God's Son! To a Muslim, this was blasphemy, but when Charlie read John 1:1, *In the beginning was the Word, and the Word was with God and the Word was God*, Tass fell to his knees as a light filled the room and a voice said, 'I am Jesus. I am the way and the truth and the life. No one comes to the Father except though me.' He blurted out, 'Jesus, come into my life. Forgive me and be my Lord and Saviour.' Peace filled his heart and God's presence was tangible.

Tass's changed lifestyle, now loving for the first time, eventually brought his wife to the Lord. He also found a love for God's chosen people – the Jews. God taught him great lessons in humility and servanthood and made him face some former giants before He led him and Karen into ministry.

Appendix 2

They founded 'Hope for Ishmael' in 2000, which aims to reconcile Jews and Arabs to the Father, then to one another. God also opened the door for Tass to preach the gospel to Arafat.

After 10 years of being cast out of his family for his conversion, and threatened with an honour killing by his brother, Tass's father finally blessed him. As Hope for Ishmael began to grow, other organizations were started. In 2005, Tass and Karen moved to Gaza and started 'Hope for Gaza': which provides education, economic development, cultural exchange and humanitarian aid to children and families in the Gaza Strip; 'Seeds of Hope': which was started in Jericho and serves the people of the West Bank; and 'Kingdom First': which serves to reconcile Jews and Arabs to Jesus; bringing hope, reconciliation, and the gospel of peace.

Now, with Hope for Ishmael primarily working out of the United States, God has given them the call to use all the experience He has given them to reach the churches in the United States and Europe. **Lead with Love** is an 8-week curriculum that was inspired from his two previous books, *Once an Arafat Man* and *Mind of Terror*, that focuses on equipping the churches with practical tools to reach our Muslim neighbours for Christ. You can learn more on their website at https://hopeforishmael.org

----

7. At Gun Point – Mitch Glaser 2017

As a teenager with a gun pointed at my head, I was forced to reassess my values in life, but it was still a long journey to find my true identity in Yeshua. I was born seven years after the Holocaust and grew up in a fairly typical 'not very religious' orthodox Jewish home. We celebrated the Jewish feasts but certainly not Christmas or Easter. We believed in one God and not three, as I thought Christians believed, and that as a Jew I could not possibly believe that God could become a man. What idolatry! If Jesus actually existed historically, then he was the saviour of the Gentiles. He couldn't be Jewish, because His followers persecuted Jews. Being Jewish was in my

All Israel Shall be Saved

blood and my soul - but not necessarily in my belief.

After my 19th birthday, I got involved in drugs and a rebellious lifestyle. I dropped out of college after one semester and went hitchhiking across the United States with a friend. While in California, I found myself at the wrong end of a double-barrel shotgun! I decided that I really did not want to risk my life for a few hundred bucks.

One of my friends became a follower of Jesus through a series of miraculous spiritual encounters. She shared her newly discovered faith which I immediately rejected. To accept the message and follow Jesus would affirm that the Jewish people were wrong about *everything*! Then my travelling companion also became a believer! To show my friends their error, I started reading my Bible - the Old Testament - and discovered that my childhood biblical heroes were great because of their faith in the God of Israel.

One day I asked God to show me the truth about Jesus. That evening, I went down to a phone booth to make a call. There I found a 'Good News for Modern Man' lit by a moonbeam in the dark. I 'stole' the book and began reading. I soon realised it was a New Testament, and that my battle was not with a non-Jew but rather with an extraordinary Jewish person who claimed to be the Messiah and God in the flesh. God smashed my objections with some extraordinary spiritual experiences that confirmed the truth and after a long struggle I accepted Yeshua. Is there anything that God cannot do? I came to believe that the Creator of the Universe is even capable of becoming a man.

Dr Mitch Glaser has served with Chosen People Ministries for almost 40 years. He has been president since 1997. He has written the book 'Isaiah 53 Explained' and initiated the 'Isaiah 53 Campaign' – a global outreach to the Jewish community.

Appendix 3: The Synagogue Readings

There are weekly Sabbath readings which cover all of Genesis to Deuteronomy (the Torah) with secondary readings from the Prophets or Writings (poetic or historical books). In addition, there are special readings for the Festivals. You can find these by searching the web under Synagogue readings. Technically, the Sephardic and Ashkenazi lists vary somewhat and there is a 3-year cycle but the website below is a Messianic one and also gives related New Testament Scriptures.
https://messianicjewish.net/media/wysiwyg/Scripture_Readings.pdf

The High Holiday Season

Some of our readers may wish to follow the Scriptures that are being read in the synagogues during this period. Rosh HaShanah is the Feast of Trumpets or Jewish New Year, which is the first day of our prayer period. It is celebrated for two days in Israel. Yom Kippur is the Day of Atonement – Day 10 of the High Holy Days. Sukkot is the Feast of Tabernacles on Day 15. Hoshana Rabbah is the last day of Sukkot – Day 21 and Shemini Atzeret is Day 22. Simchat Torah is celebrated on the same day as Shemini Atzeret in Israel but usually the day after in the diaspora. The Sabbaths are the readings for the Saturdays.

Parashat is simply the portion from the scroll which is to be read as part of the annual cyclical Biblical readings in the synagogues. The Torah is the reading from the Pentateuch (first five books of the Bible) and the Haftarah is a passage from the remainder of the Old Testament.

All Israel Shall be Saved

Parashat	Torah	Haftarah
Rosh Hashanah, Day 1	Gen 21:1-34	1 Sam 1:1-2:10
Rosh Hashanah, Day 2	Gen 22:1-24	Jeremiah 31:1-19
Shabbat Shuvah	Deut 32: 1-47	Hos 14:2-10, Mic 7:18-20
Yom Kippur, Morning	Lev 16:1-34	Isaiah 57:14-58:14
Yom Kippur, Afternoon	Lev 18:1-30	Jonah 1:1-4:11, Mic 7:18-20
Sukkot, Day 1	Lev 22:26-23:44	Zech 14:1-21
Sukkot, Day 2	Lev 22:26-23:44	1 Kings 8:2-21
Sukkot, Intermed Shabbat	Ex 33:12-34:26	Ezek 38:18-39:16
Hoshanah Rabbah	Num 29:26-34	
Shemini Atzeret	Deut 14:22-16:17	1 Kings 8:54-9:1
Simkhat Torah	Deut 33:1-34:12 Gen 1:1-2:3	Josh 1:1-18

Appendix 4: Recommended Resources

Jewish Roots

- Cahn, J., *The Book of Mysteries*, FrontLine, 2016. https://www.koorong.com
- Fruchtenbaum, A., *Jesus was a Jew*, https://www.celebratemessiah.com.au A number of Dr Fruchtenbaum's teachings are available for free downloads: http://www.ariel.org.au
- Howard, K. and Rosental, M., *The Feasts of the Lord*, Zion's Hope Inc., Orlando, 1997. https://www.celebratemessiah.com.au
- Juster, D., *Jewish Roots*. Destiny Image, Shippenburg PA, 199 (ebook). https://www.koorong.com
- Wilson, M., *Our Father Abraham: Jewish Roots of the Christian Faith*, Eerdmans Pub Co, 1989. https://www.giftsfortheking.com.au

Israel in Scripture

- Glashouwer, W., *Why Israel?*, Christians for Israel Int, 2012, https://www.giftsfortheking.com.au
- Glashouwer, W., *Why Jerusalem?* Christians for Israel Int, 2015 https://www.giftsfortheking.com.au
- Goll, J., *The Coming Israel Awakening* https://www.koorong.com (ebook)
- Prince, D., *Prophetic Guide to the End Times*, Chosen, https://www.koorong.com
- Prince, D., *The Key to the Middle East*, Chosen, 2013 https://www.koorong.com

Praying for Israel

- Hess, T., (assisted by Jill Curry), *Prepare the Way for the King of Glory*, Progressive Vision International, 2001. Materials2@jhopfan.org

Videos of Israeli Pastors

Mount Moriah Trust videos of Pastors being assisted.

All Israel Shall be Saved

- Part 1 https://www.youtube.com/watch?v=JcW2ipogivA,
- Part 2 https://www.youtube.com/watch?v=_F3kPajUFZA
- Part 3 https://www.youtube.com/watch?v=-y0DT9l4NQ8

Understanding our Times

- Cahn, J., T*he Oracle – The Jubilean Mysteries Unveiled*, Frontline, Florida, 2019 https://www.koorong.com
- Cahn, J., T*he Mystery of the Shemitah*, Frontline, Florida, 2014 https://www.koorong.com
- Glashouwer, W., *Why End Times?*, Christians for Israel Int, 2012 https://www.giftsfortheking.com.au
- Mitchell, C., *Dateline Jerusalem*, Nelson, 2013 https://www.giftsfortheking.com.au
- Tsukahira, P., *God's Tsunami: Understanding Israel and End-time Prophecy* https://www.petertsukahira.com/books

News and Prayer Information

- Bridges for Peace https://www.bridgesforpeace.com
- Christian Friends of Israel http://cfijerusalem.org/web
- Christians for Israel https://www.c4israel.org, https://www.facebook.com/c4israelAUS
- Intercessors for the Restoration of Israel http://www.out-of-zion.com
- International Christian Embassy Jerusalem https://int.icej.org, https://icej.org.au
- Jerusalem House of Prayer for All Nations Email: ancj@jhopfan.org
- Kehila News from Israel and Messianic directory https://news.kehila.org

DVD

- Crombie, K., *Gallipoli – The Road to Jerusalem* https://www.heritageresources.com.au
- Crombie, K., *October 31, Destiny's Date*, https://heritageresources.com.au
- Kitson, H., *Jerusalem, the Covenant City..* https://www.koorong.com

Appendix 4

Television

- The God TV channel also has much on Israel. https://www.god.tv/live-us
- https://sidroth.org has TV programs and other materials.

Music

- Messianic music available from https://www.giftsfortheking.com.au

Organisations assisting Aliya

- Operation Exodus http://www.operation-exodus.org
- Christians Care International https://www.christianscare.org

Outreach Tools

- Bock, D. and Glaser, M, *The Gospel according to Isaiah 53*. https://www.celebratemessiah.com.au
- Glaser, M., Isaiah 53 Explained, https://www.celebratemessiah.com.au
- Damkani, J., *Why Me?* Trumpet of Salvation, 1997 https://trumpetofsalvation.org/shop/why-me-by-jacob-damkani

The Israeli/Palestinian Conflict

- Peters, J., *From Time Immemorial*, J. KAP Pub, USA, 2000 https://www.amazon.com/Time-Immemorial-Arab-Jewish-Conflict-Palestine/dp/0963624202 Much of the information from this classic research is available on the web at https://from-time-immemorial.org

Reconciliation – Jewish/Christian

- Brown, M., *Our Hands Are Stained With Blood, The Tragic Story of the "Church" and the Jewish People*. 1992. https://www.celebratemessiah.com.au
- Finto, D., *Your People Shall be My People*, 2001 https://www.koorong.com

All Israel Shall be Saved

Tours & Information about the Land

- CMJ Australia-NZ – Martin Weatherston Tel 0417 172 205 http://cmj.org.au
- Olive Tree Travel – Steven Green http://www.olivetreetravel.com.au, steven@olivetreetravel.com.au
- Shekinah Tours – Julie Roche http://www.shekinahtours.com.au, julie@shekinahtours.com.au
- Shoresh Tours – Christ Church, Jerusalem https://www.cmj-israel.org/shoresh-tours

Websites

- Celebrate Messiah. https://www.celebratemessiah.com.au This site has a bookshop with many Messianic resources.
- Jews for Jesus. http://www.jewsforjesus.org.au Bookshop: Bondi Junction, Sydney. Tel 02-9388 0559
- Kehila News from Israel and Messianic directory https://news.kehila.org
- Information about the Feast Dates http://aroodawakening.tv/biblical-hebrew-calendar

Australia/New Zealand and Israel

- Crombie, K., *Anzacs and Israel – A Significant Connection*, Westprint Management, 2011, https://www.heritageresources.com.au
- Crombie, K., *Gallipoli to Jerusalem*, Heritage Resources, WA, 2014 https://www.giftsfortheking.com.au
- Curry, J., *The Anzac Call*, Willdeer, 2016, https://www.giftsfortheking.com.au https://www.koorong.com

Jewish & Israel Prayer Focus

International Coordinators

New Zealand

Israel Focus Group
Trish Nicholls
4 Banff Ave
Epsom
Auckland, 1023
New Zealand
Te; 09 6387789
Email: trishnicholls@xtra.co.nz

Sri Lanka

Audrey and Reggie Ebenezer
33/5 Cross Road
Alwis Town
Wattala
Sri Lanka
Tel 0094 11 2931734
Email: canaan1100@gmail.com

Papua New Guinea

Sim and D'vora Topas
JPF PNG
C/- Beit Lechem Missions Foundation Inc
PO Box 297
Maprik, ESP
Papua New Guinea
Email: baruch7hashem@gmail.com or simtopas@outlook.com

All Israel Shall be Saved

Singapore

Cheng Lai Fun
Elohim Map Kingdom Powerhouse@
CT HUB, #04-10
Kallang Bahru
Singapore 339407
Tel +65 82281835
Email: clfkingdom@yahoo.com

South Africa

Carol Clark
Republic of South Africa
Tel (27) 21 5315044
Email: restore@absamail.co.za

Other Materials by the Same Author

The Anzac Call tells the amazing story of the ANZACs story in the Middle East in WW1 and how the Allied victory led to the physical restoration of the Jewish people to their ancient land. It calls forth the spiritual Anzacs to complete the task of the spiritual restoration of the people to their God.
http://theanzaccall.com.au
Available from
http://www.giftsfortheking.com.au/ Click Books

This is a version of the above book adapted for a secular audience. It is currently out of print but the material is still available on the web at http://www.beersheba100.com.au. This includes much teaching material for schools.

Jill also researched and co-wrote this book published by the Jerusalem House of Prayer for all Nations. Available from https://jhopfan.org or email materials2@jhopfan.org

All Israel Shall be Saved

Donations for Jewish and Israel Prayer Focus

Donations to the *Jewish and Israel Prayer Focus* can be made at the following website. Click on donate button.

http://jewishandisraelprayerfocus.org

Please mark 'JIPF for Israel' or for 'JIPF General Funds'.

Israel donations go to the congregations and ministries in Israel. General Funds donations assist with our ongoing ministry running expenses.

Ministry Address: JIPF, PO Box 54, Kerrimuir, Vic 3129.

Receipts will be gladly sent upon request or automatically for large donations.

Gifts for the King

We have an online shop stocking many Israeli gifts as a way of helping the Israeli economy at a time when many countries are boycotting Israeli goods. Make your next gift a unique one and support Israel.

Judaica

Dead Sea products

Oil & Perfume

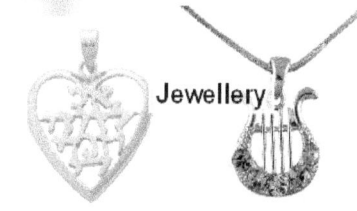
Jewellery

Banners & Flags

Books & Music

Gifts

Shofars, Prayer shawls, Messianic music, Teaching DVDs and more are available at our web site www.giftsfortheking.com.au

www.ingramcontent.com/pod-product-compliance
Lightning Source LLC
Chambersburg PA
CBHW070544010526
44118CB00012B/1213